SCENES FROM THE BIBLE

SCENES FROM THE BIBLE

WITH THE CLASSIC ILLUSTRATIONS BY

GUSTAVE DORÉ

COMPILED BY
GEORGE DAVIDSON

ARCTURUS

Images reproduced with the permission of Dover Publications

ARCTURUS

Arcturus Publishing Limited
26/27 Bickels Yard
151–153 Bermondsey Street
London SE1 3HA

Published in association with
foulsham
W. Foulsham & Co. Ltd,
The Publishing House, Bennetts Close, Cippenham,
Slough, Berkshire SL1 5AP, England

ISBN: 978-0-572-03394-1

This edition printed in 2007

British Library Cataloguing-in-Publication Data: a catalogue record for this book is available from the British Library

Typeset by MATS, Southend-on-Sea, Essex

Printed in China

Contents

Introduction

Gustave Doré was born in Strasbourg, France, in 1832 and died in Paris in 1883. In the course of his life, he became of one the best-known and most successful book illustrators of the 19th century, producing over 10,000 illustrations for more than 90 books. He was also an artist and sculptor, producing hundreds of oil paintings and watercolours and many sculptures. His fame, however, rests firmly, and justifiably, on his work as an illustrator.

Doré's career began in Paris when he was only fifteen years old. His genius was immediately recognized and his popularity quickly established, and by the age of sixteen he was already the highest-paid illustrator in France. His was a natural, in-born talent; he had no teacher, and in fact never had an art lesson in his life.

He was first employed by a Parisian publisher to draw caricatures for a humorous weekly newspaper, the *Journal pour rire*, but his attention was soon focused on book illustration. During the 1850s and 1860s, Doré illustrated some of the greatest works of world literature, among which were Dante's *Divine Comedy*, Milton's *Paradise Lost*, Cervantes' *Don Quixote* and Shakespeare's *The Tempest*. He also provided illustrations for children's classics such as the *Arabian Nights* tales, the *Fables* of La Fontaine, and Perrault's *Tales of Mother Goose*, and for travel books such as Taine's *Journey to the Waters of the Pyrenees*.

In 1865, the French publishing house of Alfred Mame et fils produced an edition of the Bible lavishly illustrated by Doré. The English-language rights to this were bought by the London publishing house of Cassell, Petter and Galpin, and *The Holy Bible, with Illustrations by Gustave Doré* was published, in parts, between 1866 and 1870, in both London and New York. Editions of the Bible with Doré's illustrations soon appeared in several other European languages.

Of the 241 plates that Doré produced to illustrate the Bible, almost all are found, in identical form, in all editions. A few plates do not appear in some editions, and there are others which appear in slightly different forms. For example, while for 'The Formation of Eve', Adam's loins are in most editions covered by a piece of cloth, as in the present book (see p. 15), an alternative version of the picture exists in which Adam's modesty is preserved not with cloth but, as with Eve, by a strategically placed plant, a solution which is more accurate from a scriptural point of view since the Bible clearly states that 'they were both naked, the man and his wife, and were not ashamed' (Genesis 2: 25).

Not all of the illustrations that appear in the present book are to be found in the 1866 Cassell edition. Of Doré's 241 Bible illustrations, only 238 are found in the English Bible (and only 228 in the original French edition). The choice of plates for the present book is based on the selection made by Millicent Rose for *The Doré Bible Illustrations* published by Dover Books in 1974. In addition to the 238 plates published in Cassell's *Holy Bible*, Rose included three plates that do not appear in the English edition, but which she took from the German edition published in Stuttgart by Eduard Hallberger Verlag in 1876-77. Furthermore, Rose opted to use nine plates from the Hallberger edition in preference to those of the Cassell edition, and of these nine, eight are included here.

Doré's Bible illustrations are considered by many to be his finest work. A reviewer of the day speaks of the 'intense vitality in his pictures, that gives to them a realism unapproached in the works of any other artist'. In them we see 'men and women, moved by the same passions, subject to the same infirmities, impressed by the same grandeur, cast down by the same sorrows, and elated by the same joys as ourselves'. Some critics at the time criticized Doré's illustrations for being too theatrical, and theatrical many of them certainly are, but it is surely from their very theatricality that these illustrations derive their power to impress us, to move us and to inspire us.

The same reviewer mentions Doré's obvious thorough acquaintance with the texts he illustrated. While this is no doubt true, it did not prevent Doré from exercising a certain artistic licence with regard to the facts. The case of the cloth across Adam's loins in the illustration of 'The Formation of Eve' has already been mentioned. Another example can be seen in Plate 89 'Ezra reading the Law in the Hearing of the People': the Bible clearly states that 'Ezra the scribe stood upon a pulpit of wood' (Nehemiah 8: 4), but Doré has visualized him standing on stone steps, perhaps the steps of the temple itself. But these are minor criticisms, and in no way detract from the force and vitality of the pictures themselves.

In selecting the 180 illustrations for the present book from the 241 available to us, the following criteria were applied. To achieve a suitable balance between the Old Testament and the New Testament, all 81 of Doré's New Testament illustrations were retained, along with 93 of the 139 Old Testament illustrations. In addition, ten plates were selected from the 21 illustrating the books of the Apocrypha. The selection from the Old Testament and Apocrypha illustrations was made mainly on the basis of how well-known and/or important were the scenes and characters depicted, but secondly on the rather more subjective basis of how interesting or appealing the illustrations were. (For example, it was the magnificent elephant in the illustration accompanying 'The Death of Eleazar' in Plate 101 that was the main factor behind the decision to include this illustration, rather than the importance of Eleazar or the significance of his death.)

The passages of the Bible accompanying the illustrations are taken from the Authorized or King James Version of 1611. The majesty and poetry of this version of the Bible well matches the power and grandeur of Doré's illustrations. It should be noted, however, that where the Scripture passages contained more information than was required, they have been edited down and their punctuation altered where necessary.

In addition to the quotations from the Bible, each illustration is accompanied by a short commentary, describing more fully the events or characters depicted and setting them in context.

It is hoped that this new edition of Doré's Bible illustrations will continue into the 21st century the fame and popularity that Doré enjoyed in the 19th and 20th centuries, among both lovers of fine art and those for whom the Bible is the basis of their faith.

George Davidson, 2007

The Old Testament

The thirty-nine books of the Old Testament contain history, law, prophecy, philosophy and poetry. Through them we can trace the story of the Jewish people from the creation of the universe to about the 5th century BC, though some of the writings are of a later date.

In the pages of these books, we read of Adam and Eve being driven out of the Garden of Eden, and of the Flood, which only Noah and his family survived. We follow the Israelites into Egypt, and from Egypt back to Canaan, and we witness their fight to establish themselves in the Promised Land. We read the histories of their leaders and kings, and of the destruction of the kingdoms of Israel and Judah by Assyria and Babylon. The story ends with the return of the Jews to Jerusalem and the rebuilding of the temple.

In the books of the prophets, we hear the voices of men called by God to warn his Chosen People of the consequences of their evil-doing, but equally to remind them of his love and mercy and his constant willingness to forgive those who repent and turn to him again. And in the Book of Job, we have a timeless meditation on suffering and God's justice and power.

The names of many of the great characters we find in the Old Testament stories – Adam and Eve, Cain and Abel, Noah, Abraham, Moses, David and Goliath, Solomon, Daniel, Jonah, Job – are familiar to us all, even to those who are not familiar with the Bible itself. (In the Bible quotation on p. 30, the name Abraham appears in its earlier form 'Abram'.)

The better to tell the story of the Jewish people as it is brought to us in the Old Testament, the illustrations in this book depict characters and events not in their Biblical order but in historical order. The Old Testament section ends with the timeless story of Job and the story of Jonah which, although bearing the name of a prophet of the 8th century BC, was almost certainly written at a later date.

The Creation of Light

And God said, Let there be light: and there was light. And God saw the light, that it was good: and God divided the light from the darkness.

(Genesis 1: 3–4)

In the story of creation, the universe is created in six days.

On the first day, God creates the heavens and the earth, but the earth is formless and empty, and everything is covered in darkness. Then God says: 'Let there be light'. And light appears. And God separates the light from the darkness, calling the light 'day' and the darkness 'night'.

The Formation of Eve

She shall be called Woman, because she was taken out of Man.

(Genesis 2: 23)

God takes some soil from the ground, forms the first man, Adam, and breathes life into him. God then creates the Garden of Eden, which Adam is to guard and cultivate.

However, God realizes that it is not good for Adam to be alone, and that the birds and animals are not adequate companions and helpers for him. So God causes Adam to fall asleep and takes out one of his ribs, from which he forms Eve, the first woman.

G. Doré

Adam and Eve Driven out of Eden

He placed at the east of the garden of Eden Cherubim, and a flaming sword which turned every way, to keep the way of the tree of life.

(GENESIS 3: 24)

God tells Adam and Eve that they can eat the fruit of any tree in the Garden of Eden except the fruit of the 'tree of the knowledge of good and evil'. However, Eve is persuaded by a serpent to eat the fruit of this tree, and to give some to Adam to eat as well.

When God realizes that Adam and Eve have eaten the forbidden fruit, he expels them from the Garden. He stations cherubim as guards to prevent Adam and Eve returning to Eden, and a flaming sword to keep them away from the 'tree of life'.

Cain and Abel Offering Their Sacrifices

Abel was a keeper of sheep, but Cain was a tiller of the ground. And Cain brought of the fruit of the ground an offering unto the Lord, and Abel brought of the firstlings of his flock.

(GENESIS 4: 2–4)

Cain and Abel are the first sons of Adam and Eve. Cain is a farmer and Abel is a shepherd. They both bring offerings to God: Cain brings some of his crops and Abel selects an offering from the first of his lambs. God accepts Abel's offering but rejects Cain's, which makes Cain very angry.

G. Doré
PANNEMAKER SC.

The Death of Abel

When they were in the field, Cain rose up against Abel his brother, and slew him. And the Lord said unto Cain, Where is Abel thy brother? And he said, I know not: Am I my brother's keeper?

(Genesis 4: 8–9)

Cain and Abel bring offerings to God. God accepts Abel's offering but rejects Cain's. Possibly as a result of the anger and jealousy he feels at this rejection, Cain one day attacks and kills his brother.

As punishment for the murder of Abel, God decrees that the ground will no longer bear crops for Cain and that he will from then on be 'a fugitive and a vagabond'. Cain spends the rest of his life a wanderer in the lands to the east of Eden.

The World Destroyed by Water

And the Lord said, I will destroy man whom I have created from the face of the earth; both man, and beast, and the creeping thing, and the fowls of the air; for it repenteth me that I have made them. But Noah found grace in the eyes of the Lord.

(Genesis 6: 7–8)

Several generations after Cain and Abel, the world has become a place of wickedness and violence and, regretting his creation, God resolves to kill every living creature on earth, both people and animals. But one righteous man and his family are to be spared: Noah, his wife, their three sons and their wives.

God instructs Noah to build a large boat so that when the flood comes to destroy the whole of creation, Noah and his family will be saved. When the boat is built, God tells Noah to take his family on board, and with them seven pairs of every species of bird and of certain species of animal, and one pair of every other species of living creature.

Seven days later, the flood begins.

The Deluge

And every living substance was destroyed which was upon the face of the ground, both man, and cattle, and the creeping things, and the fowl of the heaven; and they were destroyed from the earth: and Noah only remained alive, and they that were with him in the ark.

(Genesis 7: 23)

When the flood begins, water pours out of the ground and rain falls from the sky. It rains for forty days and forty nights, and the flood waters rise until even the highest mountains are covered to a depth of seven metres. Every human being and living creature on the earth dies.

But the ark floats safely on the surface of the water. Noah and his family and the animals and birds they gathered into the ark all survive the flood.

The Dove Sent Forth from the Ark

Again he sent forth the dove out of the ark; and the dove came in to him in the evening; and, lo, in her mouth was an olive leaf pluckt off: so Noah knew that the waters were abated from off the earth.

(Genesis 8: 10–11)

The rain stops and the flood water begins to subside, and the ark comes to rest in the mountains of Ararat. As the waters continue to go down, other mountain tops become visible.

Noah sends out a dove to see how far the water has receded. The dove comes back to the ark because the land is still covered in water. Seven days later, Noah sends out the dove again, and this time it comes back with a fresh olive leaf in its beak, so Noah knows that the water has now gone down.

After waiting another seven days, Noah sends out the dove again, and this time it does not come back. Noah looks out, and sees that the ground is drying out. Two months later, the ground is completely dry.

The Confusion of Tongues

And they said, Let us build us a city and a tower, whose top may reach unto heaven.

(Genesis 11: 4)

After the flood, all the people on earth are descendants of Noah through his three sons, Ham, Shem and Japheth. And everyone speaks the same language.

As the people migrate eastwards, they come to a plain in Babylonia. There they decide to build a city, with a tower that will reach the sky.

This plan displeases God. Therefore, in order to prevent everyone from working together to build the tower, he causes them to begin to speak different languages so that they can neither understand nor co-operate with one another.

And then God causes the human race to be scattered over the whole earth.

G. DORÉ

Abraham Journeying into the Land of Canaan

Now the Lord had said unto Abram, Get thee out of thy country, and from thy kindred, and from thy father's house, unto a land that I will shew thee: and I will make of thee a great nation, and I will bless thee, and make thy name great.

(Genesis 12: 1–2)

Along with his wife Sarah, his father Terah and his nephew Lot, Abraham leaves the city of Ur in Babylonia to travel to Canaan. But when they reach the city of Haran, they stop and settle there, and there Terah dies.

Then God says to Abraham: 'Leave Haran and your father's family, and go into the land that I will show you. And I will make you a great nation.' So when Abraham is seventy-five years old, he and his wife Sarah leave Haran with all their possessions and livestock and servants, and set out for Canaan. And Lot goes with them.

When they reach Shechem in Canaan, God appears to Abraham, and says to him: 'I will give this land to your descendents.'

Abraham and the Three Angels

And he said, Sarah thy wife shall have a son.

(GENESIS: 18: 10)

One day, as Abraham is sitting at the entrance of his tent, he sees three men standing close by. He runs to welcome them, and bowing down in front of them offers in hospitality to wash their feet and have food prepared for them. Abraham does not realize that he is talking to the Lord himself.

Although Abraham and Sarah are both very old, God promises Abraham that at a time appointed, Sarah will bear him a son. And indeed Sarah does become pregnant, and gives birth to a son, whom Abraham names Isaac.

The Flight of Lot

Then the Lord rained upon Sodom and upon Gomorrah brimstone and fire out of heaven; and he overthrew those cities, and all the plain, and all the inhabitants of the cities. But Lot's wife looked back from behind him, and she became a pillar of salt.

(Genesis 19: 24–26)

Needing more land for their flocks and herds, Abraham and Lot part company. Abraham stays in Canaan, and Lot settles near the city of Sodom in the Jordan valley.

Sodom and the nearby city of Gomorrah are renowned for their wickedness. So wicked are their inhabitants that God decides to destroy both cities; but first he sends angels to warn Lot to gather his family together and flee. Lot warns his sons-in-law of what is to come, but they do not believe him. So Lot, his wife and his two daughters flee to the town of Zoar, which the angels have promised not to destroy. Then brimstone and fire rain down, and utterly destroy Sodom and Gomorrah.

The angels have warned Lot that when he and his family flee, they must not look back. But Lot's wife does look back at the scene of destruction, and turns into a pillar of salt.

The Expulsion of Ishmael and His Mother

And Abraham rose up early in the morning, and took bread, and a bottle of water, and gave it unto Hagar, putting it on her shoulder, and the child, and sent her away.

(GENESIS 21: 14)

Believing that she cannot give Abraham a child, Sarah suggests that he should father a child by Hagar, her Egyptian slave-girl. A son is born, and Abraham names him Ishmael.

Some years later, Abraham and Sarah's own son, Isaac, is born. One day, Sarah sees Ishmael making fun of Isaac, and persuades Abraham that Hagar and Ishmael must leave. So, early the next day, Abraham gives Hagar some bread and some water and sends her away with her son.

Hagar and Ishmael in the Wilderness

And the angel of God called to Hagar: Fear not. Arise, lift up the lad, and hold him in thine hand; for I will make him a great nation. And God opened her eyes, and she saw a well of water.

(GENESIS 21: 17–19)

Abraham is persuaded by Sarah to send Hagar and Ishmael away.

After they leave the camp, they wander for some time in the wilderness. Eventually all their water is gone, and in despair Hagar puts Ishmael down in the shade of a bush and goes away so that she will not have to watch him die. But God shows Hagar a well. She fills her water bottle and gives Ishmael some water to drink.

God promises Hagar that Ishmael's descendants will become a great nation. When Ishmael grows up, he marries an Egyptian girl and has twelve sons.

The Trial of Abraham's Faith

And God said, Take now thy son, thine only son Isaac, and get thee into the land of Moriah; and offer him there for a burnt offering upon one of the mountains which I will tell thee of. And Abraham took the wood of the burnt offering, and laid it upon Isaac his son; and he took the fire in his hand, and a knife; and they went both of them together.

(Genesis 22: 2, 6)

Isaac is Abraham and Sarah's only son, the son through whom Abraham is expecting to have many descendants. But one day, God tells Abraham to take his son to Moriah and to offer him up as a sacrifice.

Abraham and Isaac travel for three days to the place that God has indicated for the sacrifice to be performed, but just as Abraham is about to kill his son, God tells him to stay his hand. He does not want Isaac to be sacrificed, he has just been testing Abraham's faith.

Then Abraham sees a ram caught by its horns in a bush nearby. He takes the ram and sacrifices it in place of his son.

Eliezer and Rebekah

The damsel was very fair to look upon; and she went down to the well and filled her pitcher.

(Genesis 24: 16)

Abraham is very old, and he wants to find a wife for his son Isaac; she must not be a Canaanite woman, however, but a girl from among his relatives still living in Mesopotamia.

So Abraham sends his servant Eliezer to Aram-naharaim where the family of Abraham's brother Nahor live. When he reaches the city of Haran, Eliezer stops beside a well, just as the women of the city are coming out to fetch water.

Among the women is Nahor's granddaughter Rebekah. When she offers Eliezer water to drink, and water for his camels, he knows that this is the girl Isaac is to marry.

Isaac Blessing Jacob

And Jacob went near unto Isaac his father; and he felt him, and said, The voice is Jacob's voice, but the hands are the hands of Esau. And he discerned him not, because his hands were hairy, as his brother Esau's hands: so he blessed him.

(Genesis 27: 22–23)

Isaac and Rebekah have two sons, Esau and Jacob. They are twins, but Esau is the firstborn. Esau is Isaac's favourite, but Rebekah favours Jacob.

When it comes to the time when Esau, as the elder son, should receive Isaac's blessing, Rebekah and Jacob trick Isaac into giving his blessing to Jacob instead. Jacob puts on some of Esau's clothes, and since Esau is a hairier man than Jacob, Rebekah covers his hands, arms and neck with the skins of young goats.

Because Isaac is nearly blind, he does not realize which of his two sons has come to him. Jacob twice assures his father that he is indeed Esau. Isaac smells Esau's clothes and feels the hairiness of Jacob's hands, and believing Jacob to be Esau, gives him the blessing that Esau should have received.

Jacob's Dream

And he dreamed, and behold a ladder set up on the earth, and the top of it reached to heaven: and behold the angels of God ascending and descending on it. And, behold, the Lord stood above it.

(Genesis 28: 12–13)

Isaac does not want Jacob to marry a Canaanite woman, but rather to marry one of the daughters of Laban, his uncle. So Jacob sets off for Haran in Mesopotamia, where Laban's family are living.

On the way, Jacob has a dream one night in which he sees a stairway stretching up to heaven. There are angels going up and down the stairway, and at the very top of it stands the Lord.

The Lord promises Jacob that the land he is on will belong to him and his descendants, who will be as numerous as the particles of dust on the ground and will spread out to north, south, east and west and bring a blessing to the whole world.

Jacob Wrestling with the Angel

And there wrestled a man with him until the breaking of the day. And he said unto him, What is thy name? And he said, Jacob. And he said, Thy name shall be called no more Jacob, but Israel.

(Genesis 32: 24, 27–28)

After working for his uncle Laban for fourteen years, and marrying Laban's daughters Leah and Rachel, Jacob is returning to Canaan.

One night, during his journey home, Jacob finds himself alone, having sent his family and his servants on ahead. A man comes and wrestles with him until dawn breaks, and only prevails over Jacob by putting his hip out of joint.

Jacob realizes that it is no man he has wrestled with, but the Angel of God, or God himself. It is God who has given him his new name, Israel.

The Meeting of Jacob and Esau

And Esau ran to meet him, and embraced him, and fell on his neck, and kissed him: and they wept.

(Genesis 33: 4)

Jacob and his mother Rebekah tricked Jacob and Esau's father Isaac into giving Jacob the blessing that should by right have been Esau's. Jacob then left Canaan to seek a wife among the daughters of his uncle Laban.

Fourteen years on, Jacob is now returning home to Canaan, and is worried about how he will be received by Esau. But Esau has forgiven his brother and is delighted to see him again.

Joseph Sold by his Brethren

They drew and lifted up Joseph out of the pit, and sold Joseph to the Ishmeelites for twenty pieces of silver: and they brought Joseph into Egypt.

(Genesis 37: 28)

Joseph has eleven brothers, but he is his father Jacob's favourite. His brothers hate him for this, and plan to kill him and tell their father that he has been eaten by a wild animal. Instead of killing him, however, they throw him into an empty well to die.

Just then, some traders come by on their way to Egypt. Joseph's brothers lift him out of the well and sell him to the traders, who take Joseph with them to Egypt, where he is sold as a slave to Potiphar, the captain of the Pharaoh's palace guard.

G. Doré

Joseph Interpreting Pharaoh's Dream

And Joseph said unto Pharaoh, The dream of Pharaoh is one: God hath shewed Pharaoh what he is about to do.

(Genesis 41: 25)

Joseph is the slave of Potiphar, the captain of the Pharaoh's guard. One night, the Pharaoh dreams that he is standing beside the River Nile when out of the river come seven fat cows and seven thin cows. The seven thin cows eat the fat cows. Then the Pharaoh has another dream, in which he sees seven plump ears of corn and seven withered ears. And the seven withered ears eat up the plump ears.

No one among the Pharaoh's wise men and magicians can interpret these dreams, so he calls for Joseph, who has already, through God's power, interpreted the dreams of two of the Pharaoh's servants. Joseph explains to the Pharaoh that the seven plump cows and ears of corn represent seven coming years of plenty, while the seven thin cows and withered ears of corn represent seven years of famine that will follow the years of plenty.

G. Doré
PANNEMAKER

Joseph Makes Himself Known to His Brethren

And Joseph said unto his brethren, Come near to me, I pray you. And they came near. And he said, I am Joseph your brother, whom ye sold into Egypt.

(Genesis 45: 4)

Joseph, once a slave, is now the governor of the whole of Egypt. Famine brings Joseph's brothers down from Canaan to Egypt to buy grain, since thanks to Joseph's wise preparations, the Egyptians have more than enough grain to survive the famine.

Joseph's brothers do not recognize him, but he recognizes them at once. At first he conceals his identity from them, but eventually he reveals to them who he is. He explains to his brothers that although it was they who sold him as a slave, it was in fact all part of God's plan for him to go to Egypt to ensure that there would be food for his family when the famine came.

Jacob Goeth into Egypt

And Jacob rose up from Beersheba: and the sons of Israel carried Jacob their father, and their little ones, and their wives, in the wagons which Pharaoh had sent to carry him. And they took their cattle, and their goods, and came into Egypt.

(Genesis 46: 5–6)

During a famine, Joseph's brothers have gone down to Egypt to buy grain, and Joseph has revealed his identity to them. Since there are still years of famine ahead, Joseph suggests to his brothers that they bring their father Jacob and their families down to Egypt, where the Pharaoh has promised to give them some of the best land in the country.

Jacob is overjoyed to learn that his son Joseph is alive, and the whole family sets off for Egypt. On the way south, Jacob stops at Beersheba to offer sacrifices to God. God speaks to Jacob in a vision, promising him that his family will become a great nation in Egypt and that they will then be brought back to Canaan again.

G. Doré

The Child Moses on the Nile

And when she could not longer hide him, she took for him an ark of bulrushes, and put the child therein; and she laid it in the flags by the river's brink.

(Exodus 2: 3)

The descendants of Joseph and his brothers have grown into a great nation in Egypt. Feeling threatened by this foreign people in their midst, the Egyptians turn on the Israelites and make them their slaves. But still the Israelites grow in number. So the Pharaoh gives orders that all male Israelite babies are to be killed at birth.

When Moses is born, his mother hides him for three months. But when she can no longer hide him, she places him in a reed basket, which she has waterproofed with tar and pitch, and lays the basket in reeds close to the riverbank.

Moses' sister watches to see what will happen.

The Finding of Moses

And the daughter of Pharaoh came down to wash herself at the river; and when she saw the ark among the flags, she sent her maid to fetch it. And when she had opened it, she saw the child. And she had compassion on him, and said, This is one of the Hebrews' children.

(Exodus 2: 5–6)

To avoid him being killed, Moses' mother hides her baby son in a basket in reeds close to the riverbank. When the Pharaoh's daughter comes down to the river to bathe, she sees the basket and sends her maid to bring it to her.

The princess realizes at once that the baby is an Israelite baby, but it is crying and she takes pity on it. Moses' sister approaches her and offers to find a wet nurse for the baby. She agrees, and Moses' sister fetches her mother. The princess gives Moses' mother the baby to look after.

When the boy is old enough, the Pharaoh's daughter adopts him as her son, and names him Moses.

G. Doré
PANNEMAKER

Moses and Aaron before Pharaoh

And Aaron cast down his rod before Pharaoh, and before his servants, and it became a serpent.

(Exodus 7: 10)

When Moses is a young man, he kills an Egyptian, and flees to Midian. There one day God speaks to him out of a burning bush, and tells him that he will rescue the Israelites from their slavery in Egypt and bring them back to Canaan.

Moses returns to Egypt, and he and his brother Aaron go to the Pharaoh to ask him to allow the Israelites to leave. (Moses is by this time eighty years old.) As a sign of God's power, Aaron throws down his staff and it turns into a snake. The Pharaoh's magicians do the same, but when their staffs turn into snakes, Aaron's snake swallows them up.

The Murrain of Beasts

For if thou refuse to let them go, and wilt hold them still, behold, the hand of the Lord is upon thy cattle, upon the horses, upon the asses, upon the camels, upon the oxen, and upon the sheep: there shall be a very grievous murrain.

(Exodus 9: 2–3)

When Moses and Aaron ask the Pharaoh to allow the Israelites to leave Egypt, he refuses. To change the Pharaoh's mind, God brings down ten plagues on the Egyptians.

The first plague causes the water of the Nile to turn to blood. Next comes a plague of frogs, followed by a plague of gnats and then a plague of flies.

The fifth plague is a plague of disease, which kills the Egyptians' livestock.

The Plague of Darkness

And the Lord said unto Moses, Stretch out thine hand toward heaven, that there may be darkness over the land of Egypt. And Moses stretched forth his hand toward heaven; and there was a thick darkness in all the land of Egypt three days.

(Exodus 10: 21–22)

In order to persuade the Egyptian Pharaoh to allow the Israelites to leave Egypt, God sends down ten plagues on the Egyptian people.

The ninth plague is total darkness, which lasts for three days. There is no light in Egypt, but the Israelites have light in their dwellings.

The Firstborn Slain

And it came to pass, that at midnight the Lord smote all the firstborn in the land of Egypt. There was not a house where there was not one dead.

(Exodus 12: 29–30)

The final plague that God sends down on the Egyptians is the death of the firstborn son of every family in Egypt. In order to spare the Israelite children, God tells Moses that Israelite families must kill a lamb or a young goat and smear its blood on their doorframes.

When the Angel of Death passes over the land, killing the firstborn sons of the Egyptians, he does not enter any house that is marked in this way, and so the Israelite children are spared.

G. Doré

The Egyptians Urge Moses to Depart

And he called for Moses and Aaron by night, and said, Rise up, and get you forth from among my people, both ye and the children of Israel; and go, serve the Lord, as ye have said.

(Exodus 12: 31)

The tenth plague that God sends down upon the Egyptians breaks the Pharaoh's resistance. He sends for Moses and Aaron and orders them and all the Israelites to leave Egypt, along with their flocks and herds. The Egyptians urge the Israelites to leave as quickly as possible, before God sends down yet another plague on them.

The Egyptians Drowned in the Red Sea

And Moses stretched forth his hand over the sea, and the waters returned, and covered the chariots, and the horsemen, and all the host of Pharaoh that came into the sea after them; there remained not so much as one of them.

(Exodus 14: 27–28)

After allowing the Israelites to leave Egypt, the Pharaoh regrets letting them go. He sets out with his army in hot pursuit, and catches up with them beside the Red Sea. The Israelites are very afraid, but Moses assures them that God will come to their aid.

God tells Moses to hold out his hand over the water. Moses does so, and a strong wind blows up that parts the sea and allows the Israelites to cross on a dry path, between two walls of water.

The Egyptians follow the Israelites across the dry ground. God then tells Moses to stretch out his hand once again over the water. When Moses does so, the walls of water collapse over Pharaoh and his army and they are drowned.

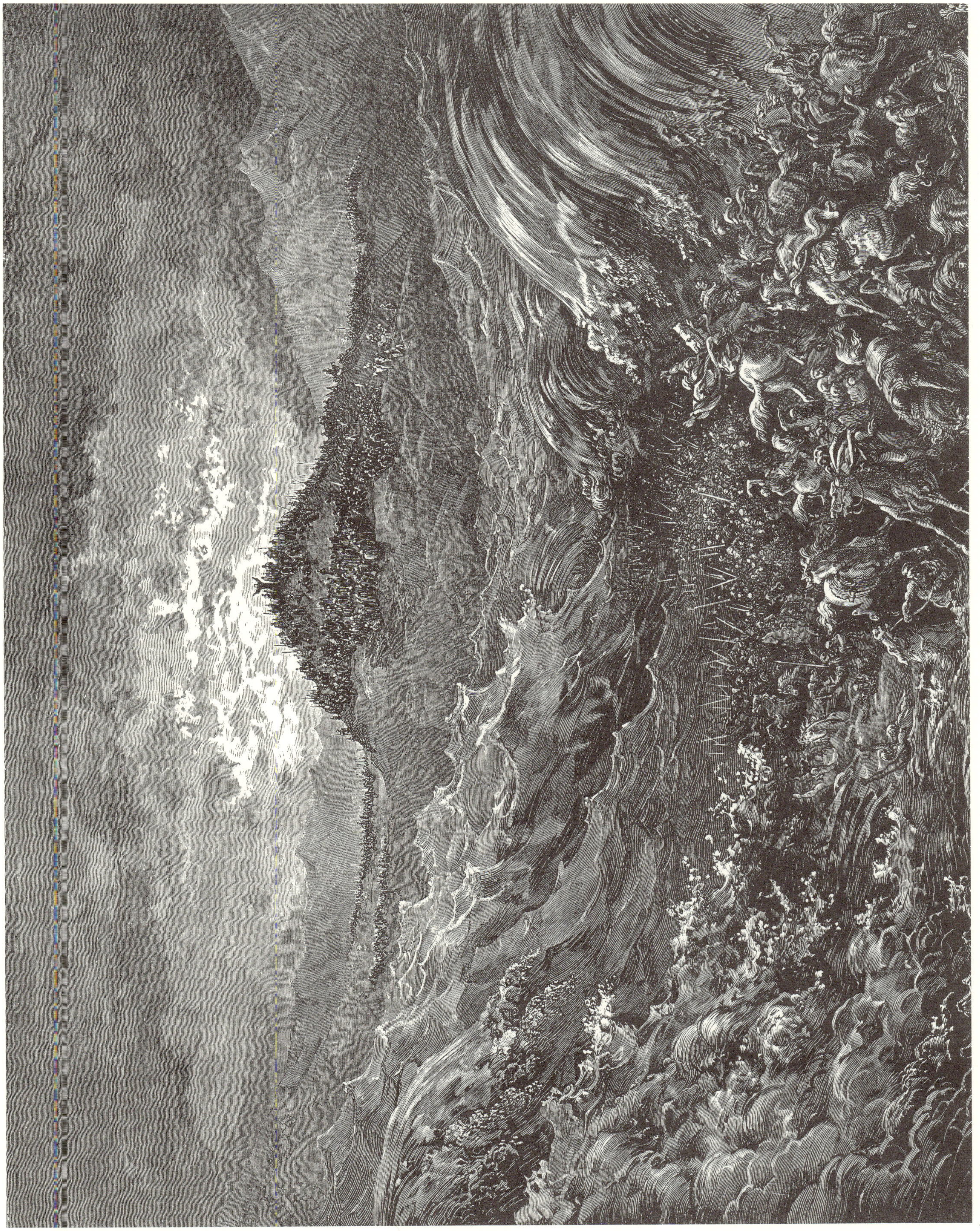

The Giving of the Law upon Mount Sinai

And it came to pass on the third day in the morning, that there were thunders and lightnings, and a thick cloud upon the mount, and the voice of the trumpet exceeding loud; so that all the people that was in the camp trembled.

(Exodus 19: 16)

Two months after leaving Egypt, the Israelites reach the Sinai Desert and set up camp at the foot of Mount Sinai.

God tells Moses that he will come to speak to him on the mountain, so that the Israelites will hear him speaking and will believe what Moses tells them.

There follow two days of purification. Then, on the third day, a thick cloud comes down over the mountain with thunder and lightening, and a loud trumpet blast is heard. Moses leads the Israelites out of their camp and they stand at the foot of the mountain. The whole mountain is shaking, and it is enveloped in smoke because God has come down to the mountain in fire.

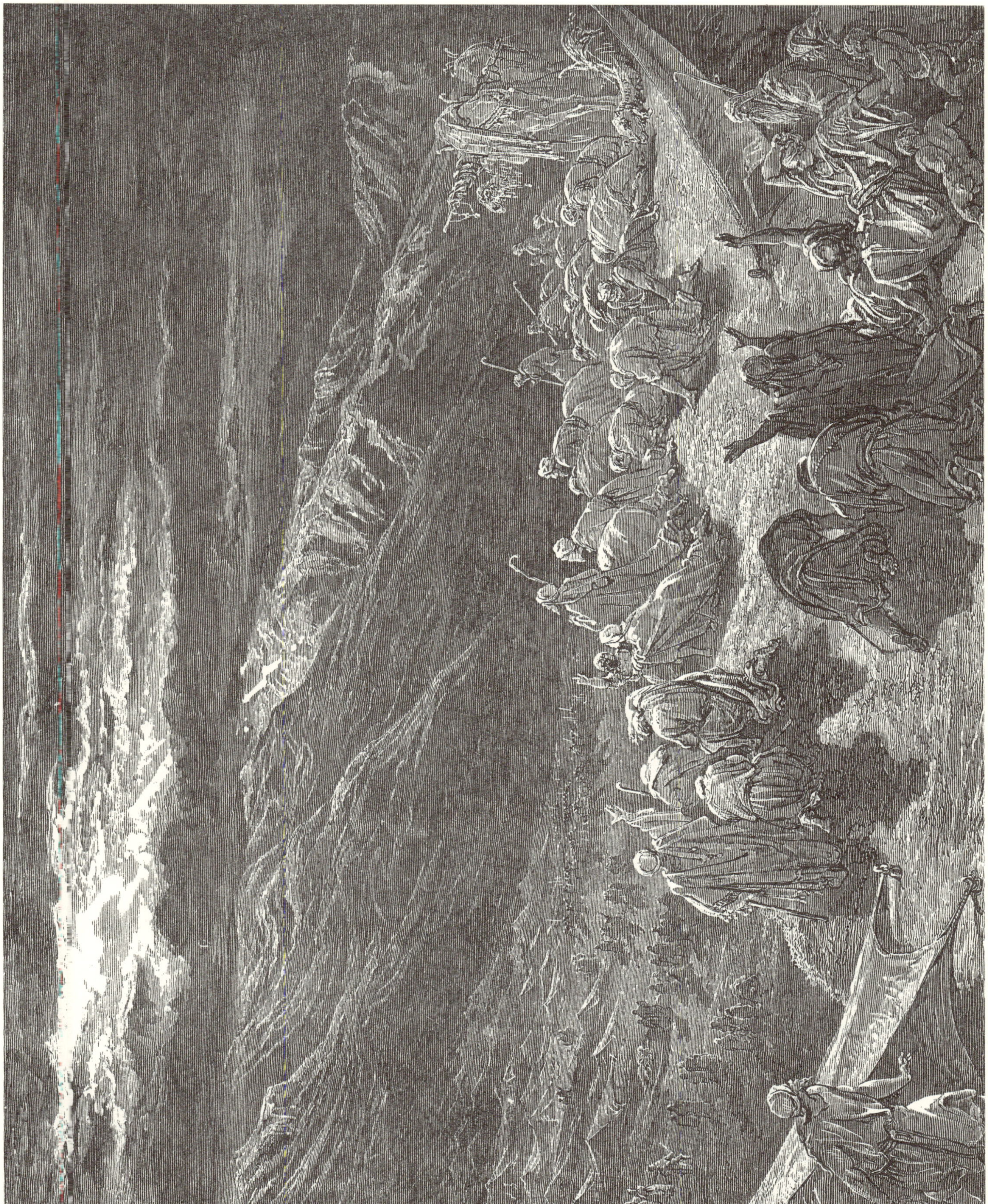

Moses Coming Down from Mount Sinai

And Moses turned, and went down from the mount, and the two tables of the testimony were in his hand: the tables were written on both their sides. And the tables were the work of God, and the writing was the writing of God, graven upon the tables.

(Exodus 32: 15–16)

God calls Moses up to the top of Mount Sinai, and there he stays for forty days and nights.

God gives Moses two stone tablets on which he has written the laws that the Israelites are to obey. At the end of the forty days, Moses returns to the Israelite camp with the stone tablets.

Moses Breaking the Tables of the Law

And it came to pass, as soon as he came nigh unto the camp, that he saw the calf, and the dancing: and Moses' anger waxed hot, and he cast the tables out of his hands, and brake them beneath the mount.

(Exodus 32: 19)

When Moses comes down from Mount Sinai with the stone tablets on which God has written the laws the Israelites are to obey, he finds that the Israelites have made a golden idol in the shape of a calf, and are worshipping it.

Moses is so angry that he throws down the stone tablets and breaks them. Then he melts down the golden calf, grinds the gold to powder, mixes it with water and forces the Israelites to drink it.

The Return of the Spies from the Land of Promise

And they came to Moses and said, We came unto the land whither thou sentest us, and surely it floweth with milk and honey; and this is the fruit of it.

(Numbers 13: 26–27)

God has promised Moses that he will lead the Israelites to a 'land flowing with milk and honey' in Canaan.

After leaving Sinai, the Israelites journey northwards till they reach the wilderness of Paran. From there, Moses sends spies into Canaan to see what the land is like and how numerous and powerful its inhabitants are.

When the spies return, they are carrying grapes, pomegranates and figs. They tell Moses and the Israelites that Canaan is indeed a 'land flowing with milk and honey'.

The Brazen Serpent

And Moses made a serpent of brass, and put it upon a pole, and it came to pass, that if a serpent had bitten any man, when he beheld the serpent of brass, he lived.

(NUMBERS 21: 9)

Still on their way to Canaan, the Israelites become discouraged because their journey to the promised land is taking so long. They begin to speak out against Moses and against God.

As punishment for this, God sends poisonous snakes in among them, and many of the people are bitten and die. When the Israelites repent of their grumbling, God tells Moses to make a brass snake, which Moses does. Thereafter, if anyone who has been bitten by a snake looks at the brass snake, they survive.

G. Doré
L. DUMONT

The Angel Appearing to Balaam

And the ass saw the angel of the Lord standing in the way, and his sword drawn in his hand: and the ass turned aside out of the way, and went into the field: and Balaam smote the ass, to turn her into the way.

(NUMBERS 22: 23)

The Israelites reach Moab, to the east of the Dead Sea. In fear, the king of Moab sends for Balaam, a prophet, to come and put a curse on the Israelites so that the Moabites can drive them out of their land.

God tells Balaam not to go to Moab and not to curse the Israelites. But when a second delegation comes from Moab to fetch him, Balaam is this time allowed to go with them. However, God then sends an angel to bar Balaam's way. Balaam cannot see the angel, but his donkey can. It turns off into a field, and is beaten by its master until it goes back onto the road again.

G. Doré

The Children of Israel Crossing Jordan

And as they that bare the ark were come unto Jordan, the waters which came down from above stood and rose up upon an heap. And the priests that bare the ark of the covenant of the Lord stood firm on dry ground in the midst of Jordan until all the people were passed clean over Jordan.

(Joshua 3: 15–17)

The Israelites reach the banks of the River Jordan, which they must cross in order to enter Canaan. By this time, Moses has died, and Joshua is the leader of the people. God tells Joshua that the priests who are carrying the ark of the covenant are to go down to the river and wade into the water.

When the priests do this, the river stops flowing and the water piles up in a mound some distance away upstream. And so the Israelites are able to cross the Jordan on dry ground. When all the people are across, the priests come out of the river and the waters begin to flow again.

The Walls of Jericho Falling Down

So the people shouted when the priests blew with the trumpets: and it came to pass, when the people heard the sound of the trumpet, and the people shouted with a great shout, that the wall fell down flat.

(JOSHUA 6: 20)

After crossing the River Jordan, the Israelites make camp close to the city of Jericho, and God explains to Joshua how they are to capture the city.

Following God's instructions, on each of the following six days the ark of the covenant is carried once round the outside of the city, behind seven priests blowing ram's-horn trumpets. On the seventh day, however, the Israelites march round the city seven times. Then the priests sound a long blast on their trumpets, all the people shout, and the walls of the city collapse. And so the Israelites capture Jericho.

The Destruction of the Army of the Amorites

And the Lord cast down great stones from heaven upon them, and they died: they were more which died with hailstones than they whom the children of Israel slew with the sword.

(Joshua 10: 11)

After the Israelites capture and destroy the cities of Jericho and Ai, the inhabitants of the city of Gibeon, fearing the same fate will befall them, trick the Israelites into making a peace treaty with them. In response to this, the Amorites lay siege to Gibeon.

The Gibeonites send word to Joshua, asking the Israelites to come to their rescue. The Israelites attack and rout the Amorite army, and as the Amorites flee, God rains stones down on them, killing even more Amorites with the stones than the Israelites have killed with their weapons.

Joshua Commanding the Sun to Stand Still

Then spake Joshua to the Lord in the day when the Lord delivered up the Amorites before the children of Israel, and he said in the sight of Israel, Sun, stand thou still upon Gibeon; and thou, Moon, in the valley of Ajalon.

(Joshua 10: 12)

On the day that God gives the Israelites their victory over the Amorites, Joshua asks God to make the sun and the moon stand still in the sky until the Israelites have completely defeated their enemies. And the sun does stand still and the moon does remain where it is. The sun stays unmoving in the middle of the sky for a whole day while the Israelites crush the Amorites.

Jael and Sisera

Then Jael Heber's wife took a nail of the tent, and took an hammer in her hand, and went softly unto him, and smote the nail into his temples, and fastened it into the ground: for he was fast asleep and weary. So he died.

(JUDGES 4: 21)

As a punishment for their sins, God allows the Israelites to be conquered by Jabin, a Canaanite king. Jabin oppresses the Israelites cruelly for 20 years.

Then, under God's guidance, Deborah, the leader of the Israelites at the time, tells Barak to gather together an army of 10,000 men. Sisera, the commander of Jabin's army, marches against Barak. In the battle that follows, the Israelites utterly rout the Canaanites. Sisera flees, and takes refuge in the tent of Jael, the wife of Heber.

While Sisera is asleep, Jael takes a tent peg and hammers it through his head. And so Sisera dies.

Gideon Choosing His Soldiers

So he brought down the people unto the water: and the Lord said unto Gideon, Every one that lappeth of the water with his tongue, as a dog lappeth, him shalt thou set by himself. And the number of them that lapped were three hundred men. And the Lord said unto Gideon, By the three hundred men that lapped will I save you, and deliver the Midianites into thine hand.

(Judges 7: 5–7)

The Israelites are being terrorized by the Midianites, the Amalekites and other desert tribes, but God tells Gideon that he will free Israel from its oppressors. Gideon then musters an army of thirty-two thousand men. But God does not want the Israelites to attack their enemies with a large army, lest they think that the victory he has promised them is due to their prowess rather than his action on their behalf.

So God tells Gideon that all those who are afraid should be allowed to go back home. Twenty-two thousand of Gideon's men do so, but this still leaves a larger Israelite army than God wants. So, to further reduce their number, God tells Gideon to watch how his men drink water. Only those who scoop up water in their hands and lap it like dogs are to remain with him.

In this way, three hundred men are chosen.

The Midianites Put to Flight

And the three companies blew the trumpets, and brake the pitchers, and held the lamps in their left hands, and the trumpets in their right hands to blow withal: and they cried, The sword of the Lord, and of Gideon.

(Judges 7: 20)

Gideon is about to the attack the Midianite camp with three hundred men. He splits his men into three companies, and gives each man a trumpet and a jar with a burning torch in it.

When Gideon and his company of men reach the enemy camp, they blow their trumpets and break the jars to reveal the burning torches. The men of the two other companies do likewise. They all shout: 'The sword of the Lord, and of Gideon'.

At this, the Midianites rush about in panic, and try to escape. God sows confusion among them, and they attack each other. Those who are not killed flee, pursued by the Israelites.

Jephthah's Daughter Coming to Meet Her Father

Jephthah vowed a vow unto the Lord, and said, If thou shalt deliver the children of Ammon into mine hands, whatsoever cometh forth of the doors of my house to meet me when I return, I will offer it up for a burnt offering. And Jephthah came unto his house, and, behold, his daughter came out to meet him: and she was his only child.

(JUDGES 11: 30–31, 34)

Once again, the Israelites sin against God, and as punishment God allows the Ammonites to oppress them. When the Israelites repent, however, God comes to their aid.

Jephthah of Gilead gathers an army together and leads it out against the Ammonites. But before the battle, he makes a vow that if God gives him the victory, he will on his return home sacrifice whoever first comes out of his house to greet him.

Returning home victorious, Jephthah is greeted by his daughter, his only child. Heartbroken, he tells her of his vow, and she insists that he must carry it out, asking only for a delay of two months so that she can wander over the mountains with her friends and mourn that she will never have children.

G. Doré
PANNEMAKER-DOM

Samson Slaying a Lion

And, behold, a young lion roared against him. And the Spirit of the Lord came mightily upon him, and he rent him as he would have rent a kid, and he had nothing in his hand.

(Judges 14: 5–6)

One day Samson, an Israelite, tells his parents that he wants to marry a certain Philistine girl, so he and his parents go together to the town of Timnah where he saw her. As they are approaching the town, a young lion roars at them.

Suddenly, through the power of God, Samson becomes very strong, and he tears the lion apart with his bare hands, just as easily as he would have torn apart a young goat.

Samson Destroying the Philistines with the Jawbone of an Ass

And he found a new jawbone of an ass, and put forth his hand, and took it, and slew a thousand men therewith.

(Judges 15: 15)

Samson has burned the Philistines' cornfields, vineyards and olive groves, and has killed many of their people. So the Philistines invade Judah and attack the town of Lehi.

When the people of Judah learn that it is really Samson the Philistines have come for, they tie him up and hand him over. Suddenly, the power of God gives Samson great strength, and he breaks the ropes he is tied with as easily as if they had been linen threads. Then he picks up the jawbone of a dead donkey that he sees lying nearby, and with it kills a thousand Philistines.

Samson and Delilah

When she pressed him daily with her words so that his soul was vexed unto death, he told her: If I be shaven, then my strength will go from me, and I shall become weak, and be like any other man.

(Judges 16: 16–17)

Through an extraordinary God-given strength, Samson has several times brought death and destruction to the Philistines. So when he falls in love with Delilah, the Philistines bribe her to persuade him to tell her the source of this strength.

Three times Samson deceives Delilah about where his strength comes from, and on each occasion she passes this incorrect information to the Philistines, who then try in vain to overpower him.

Delilah continues to press Samson to tell her what she wants to know, and eventually Samson gives in. He tells her that when he was born, he was dedicated to God, and is therefore not allowed to cut his hair. If his hair was ever cut, he would become as weak as any other man.

The Death of Samson

And Samson said, Let me die with the Philistines. And he bowed himself with all his might; and the house fell upon the lords, and upon all the people that were therein. So the dead which he slew at his death were more than they which he slew in his life.

(JUDGES 16: 30)

When Samson tells Delilah that he would lose his miraculous strength if his hair was cut, she lulls him to sleep and has his hair shaved off. When the Philistines come to capture him, Samson's strength has gone and he is unable to resist. The Philistines put out Samson's eyes and bind him with chains.

One day, when the Philistines are having a great feast, they bring Samson out of prison to make fun of him. They stand him between the pillars that support the roof of the building. But Samson prays to God for strength just one last time, and, his prayer being granted, he pushes the pillars apart and brings the building crashing down on the Philistines, killing himself as well. So Samson kills more people at the time of his death than during his whole life.

Boaz and Ruth

Boaz commanded his young men, saying, Let her glean even among the sheaves, and reproach her not: And let fall also some of the handfuls of purpose for her, and leave them, that she may glean them.

(RUTH 2: 15-16)

Ruth is the Moabite daughter-in-law of Naomi, an Israelite woman. Both of them are widows, and very poor.

One day, Boaz, a rich Bethlehem landowner and a relative of Naomi's late husband, sees Ruth gleaning grain in his fields. Learning of the women's straitened circumstances and of Ruth's loyalty to Naomi, Boaz invites her to eat with his harvest-workers, and also gives orders to the workers to deliberately leave grain in the fields for her to pick up. Ruth continues to glean in Boaz's fields until the harvest is over.

Boaz eventually marries Ruth, and they have a son, Obed, the grandfather of David, who becomes king of Israel.

The Return of the Ark to Beth-shemesh

And they of Beth-shemesh were reaping their wheat harvest in the valley: and they lifted up their eyes, and saw the ark, and rejoiced to see it.

(1 Samuel 6: 13)

In a fierce battle with the Israelites, the Philistines capture the sacred ark of the covenant. They take it to the city of Ashdod and place it in the temple of Dagon, their god.

But God severely punishes the people of Ashdod. The whole city and the surrounding villages suffer a plague of mice and a plague of tumours. So the ark is taken from Ashdod to Gath, but there too God punishes the people with a plague. From Gath, the ark is taken to Ekron, another Philistine city, but its citizens too are struck down by the plague, and many die.

So the Philistines send the ark back to the Israelites at Beth-Shemesh, along with gifts of gold in the shape of mice and tumours.

Samuel Blessing Saul

And when Samuel saw Saul, the Lord said unto him, Behold the man whom I spake to thee of! this same shall reign over my people.

(1 SAMUEL 9: 17)

The Israelites have asked the prophet Samuel to find them a king. But who is to be this king?

One day, God tells Samuel that a man will come to him the next day, and that he is the one who is to be anointed king. Meanwhile, Saul has been searching for days for his father's donkeys, which have wandered off. He is about to give up the search when his servant suggests they consult the local prophet, who might know where the donkeys are.

As Saul and his servant enter the town, they meet Samuel. And God says to Samuel: 'This is the man I told you about. This is the man who is to be the king.' And the next day, Samuel anoints Saul as king of Israel.

David and Goliath

And David put his hand in his bag, and took thence a stone, and slang it, and smote the Philistine in his forehead; and he fell upon his face to the earth. David ran, and stood upon the Philistine, and took his sword and slew him.

(1 Samuel 17: 49, 51)

The Philistine army and the Israelite army are lined up for battle on the opposite sides of a valley. Among the Philistines is Goliath, a huge man over nine feet tall, wearing bronze armour and carrying a massive spear. Goliath challenges the Israelites to pick someone to fight him in one-to-one combat, but no Israelite soldier is brave enough to accept the challenge.

However, David, a shepherd boy who is visiting his older brothers in the Israelite camp, offers to fight the giant. He picks up five smooth stones, and with his sling in his hand, he approaches Goliath. As Goliath advances on him, David slings a stone at him. The stone hits Goliath in the forehead and he falls to the ground. David runs over to the giant, draws his sword, kills him and cuts off his head. When the Philistines see their champion is dead, they flee.

Saul Attempts the Life of David

And it came to pass on the morrow, that the evil spirit from God came upon Saul, and there was a javelin in Saul's hand. And Saul cast the javelin; for he said, I will smite David even to the wall with it.

(1 Samuel 18: 10–11)

After David kills Goliath and successfully carries out other missions for Saul, the people sing his praises, saying: 'Saul has killed thousands, but David has killed tens of thousands'. This makes Saul angry and jealous.

David is not only a brave warrior but also a gifted harpist. Whenever Saul becomes depressed, David plays for him until Saul's depression lifts. One day, in a fit of madness, while David is playing the harp for him, Saul tries to kill him. He throws his spear at David, but David manages to dodge it and escape.

David and Jonathan

And Jonathan said to David, Go in peace. The Lord be between me and thee, and between my seed and thy seed for ever.

(1 Samuel 20: 42)

Jonathan is the son of Saul, the Israelite king, and in spite of his father's hatred of David, he loves David like a brother.

Although Jonathan does not at first believe that Saul wants to kill David, he tests his father and finds it to be true. So he goes out into the countryside where David is hiding, and warns him that he must flee.

David comes out of hiding, and before he leaves, Jonathan swears an oath of eternal friendship, both between himself and David and between his descendants and David's descendants.

The Combat between the Champions of Ishbosheth and David

Then there arose and went over twelve which pertained to Ishbosheth the son of Saul, and twelve of the servants of David. And they caught every one his fellow by the head, and thrust his sword in his fellow's side; so they fell down together: And there was a very sore battle that day.

(2 Samuel 2: 15–17)

After Saul's death in battle against the Philistines, his kingdom splits into two. David is anointed king of Judah and Saul's son Ishbosheth is made king of Israel.

And then war breaks out between Judah and Israel. To settle the matter, it is agreed that twelve of David's men will fight twelve men from Ishbosheth's army. When the contest begins, each of the twenty-four fighters grabs his opponent by the head and plunges his sword into his opponent's body, and all twenty-four fall down dead at the same time. A fierce battle then begins, and the army of Israel is defeated by the men of Judah.

David Punishing the Ammonites

And Joab sent messengers to David, and said, I have fought against Rabbah, and have taken the city of waters. Now therefore gather the rest of the people together, and encamp against the city, and take it: lest I take the city, and it be called after my name.

(2 Samuel 12: 27–28)

The Ammonites having needlessly insulted King David, a great battle is fought outside the Ammonite city of Rabbah between the Ammonite forces and David's army under the command of Joab.

Joab defeats the Ammonites and captures the city's water supply; but not wanting to be given the glory of capturing the city itself, he sends word to David to come to lead the army in the final stage of the campaign. Under David's leadership, the Israelites take the city, plunder it and enslave its people.

David Mourning the Death of Absalom

And the king said unto Cushi, Is the young man Absalom safe? And Cushi answered, The enemies of my lord the king, and all that rise against thee to do thee hurt, be as that young man is. And the king was much moved, and went up to the chamber over the gate, and wept: and as he went, thus he said, O my son Absalom, my son, my son Absalom! would God I had died for thee, O Absalom, my son, my son!

(2 Samuel 18: 32–33)

Absalom is a son of King David, but he leads a rebellion against his father and is anointed king by the northern tribes of Israel.

Eventually, the armies of the two kings meet in battle. During the battle, Absalom runs into some of David's men. Although David has given specific instructions that Absalom's life is to be spared if he is captured, he is killed by Joab, one of David's generals.

When David is brought the news of his son's death, he weeps.

The Judgment of Solomon

Then the king answered and said, Give her the living child, and in no wise slay it: she is the mother thereof.

(1 Kings 3: 27)

Two prostitutes bring a case to King Solomon, who is famous for his wisdom. The women live together and both have recently had a baby. According to one of the women, the other woman's baby died one night, but its mother swapped the babies over, taking the living child and leaving the dead child in the first woman's bed. In the morning, the mother of the living baby realizes what has happened, but the mother of the dead baby denies everything, claiming the living baby is truly hers.

To test the women, Solomon orders the baby to be cut in two, so that each woman can have an equal share of it. One of the women agrees, but the other woman begs the king not to kill the baby but to give it to her rival. Solomon knows that this woman must be the baby's true mother.

Cutting Down Cedars for the Construction of the Temple

And, behold, I purpose to build an house unto the name of the Lord my God. Now therefore command thou that they hew me cedar trees out of Lebanon.

(1 Kings 5: 5–6)

It distressed King David that, while he lived in a palace of cedar wood, the ark of the covenant was kept in a tent. David wanted to build a temple for the Lord, but through the prophet Nathan God told him that it was not he but one of his sons who would perform this task.

When David's son Solomon becomes king, he sets about building the temple. For this purpose, he asks Hiram, the king of Tyre, to supply him with cedar wood, because the people of Tyre are more skilled than the Israelites in cutting timber. Hiram supplies Solomon with both cedar and pine logs, which are hauled down to the sea and then formed into rafts and floated south to Israel.

Solomon Receiving the Queen of Sheba

And when the queen of Sheba heard of the fame of Solomon, she came to Jerusalem, with a very great company, and camels that bare spices, and gold in abundance, and precious stones: and when she was come to Solomon, she communed with him of all that was in her heart.

(2 Chronicles 9: 1)

King Solomon is famed for his wisdom. He is said to be wiser than all the wise men of the East and the wise men of Egypt. Hearing of Solomon's wisdom, but not believing it, the Queen of Sheba comes to Jerusalem to test him with difficult questions. But no matter what she asks Solomon, he is able to provide an answer. Nothing she asks him is too difficult for him to explain.

Elijah Raiseth the Son of the Widow of Zarephath

And Elijah took the child, and brought him down out of the chamber into the house, and delivered him unto his mother: and Elijah said, See, thy son liveth.

(1 Kings 17: 23)

While the prophet Elijah is in hiding from King Ahab of Israel, God tells him to go to Zarephath, near Sidon, where there is a widow who will feed him.

While Elijah is staying with the widow, he performs two miracles. Firstly, when she is beginning to run out of food, Elijah, through God's power, causes there to be always enough flour and oil in her jars for her to feed him, herself and her son. And then, when the widow's son falls ill and dies, Elijah prays to God that the boy be restored to life; and his prayer is answered.

The Slaughter of the Prophets of Baal

And Elijah said unto them, Take the prophets of Baal; let not one of them escape. And they took them: and Elijah brought them down to the brook Kishon, and slew them there.

(1 Kings 18: 40)

Married to Jezebel, a princess from Sidon, King Ahab of Israel abandons the Lord and worships Jezebel's god, Baal.

The prophet Elijah issues a challenge to the prophets of Baal. They will offer sacrifices to their respective gods in a way that will demonstrate who is the true god. They will each build an altar, lay wood and sacrificial meat on it, and then call on their god to set the wood alight.

Having built their altar, the prophets of Baal call on their god to set the sacrifice alight, but to no avail. Elijah then builds his altar, puts wood and meat on it, and has water poured all over it. He prays, and God answers his prayer: fire flashes down from heaven and burns everything up, even drying up all the water.

Elijah then orders the Israelites to kill all the prophets of Baal.

G. Doré
L. Dumont

Elijah Nourished by an Angel

And as he lay and slept under a juniper tree, behold, then an angel touched him, and said unto him, Arise and eat.

(1 Kings 19: 5)

The prophet Elijah has brought about the deaths of the prophets of Baal. When Queen Jezebel learns what Elijah has done, she sends a message to him saying that by the same time the next day, he will be a dead man too. So Elijah flees.

Elijah goes out into the desert, and sits down under a tree. He prays to God to let him die, as life has become more than he can bear. Then he falls asleep. While he is sleeping, an angel comes to him, and says: 'Wake up and eat something.' And when Elijah looks round, there is a loaf of bread beside him, and a jar of water.

Elijah Destroys the Messengers of Ahaziah by Fire

And Elijah answered and said to the captain of fifty, If I be a man of God, then let fire come down from heaven, and consume thee and thy fifty. And there came down fire from heaven, and consumed him and his fifty.

(2 Kings 1: 10)

King Ahaziah of Israel falls through a lattice screen, seriously injuring himself. He sends messengers to inquire of the god Baalzebub whether he will recover, but God tells the prophet Elijah to tell the messengers that Ahaziah is going to die of his injuries.

When Ahaziah hears what Elijah has said, he sends soldiers to bring the prophet to him. When the soldiers find Elijah, he calls down fire on them. A second company of soldiers is sent to fetch Elijah, and the same thing happens to them. But when a third company of soldiers is sent to Elijah, the officer begs the prophet to spare them. And God tells Elijah to go with them to the king.

Elijah Taken Up to Heaven in a Chariot of Fire

Behold, there appeared a chariot of fire, and horses of fire, and parted them both asunder; and Elijah went up by a whirlwind into heaven. And Elisha saw it, and he cried, My father, my father, the chariot of Israel, and the horsemen thereof. And he saw him no more.

(2 Kings 2: 11–12)

The prophet Elijah is about to die. Elijah and Elisha go down to the River Jordan. Wanting to cross the river, Elijah strikes the river with his cloak; the waters of the river part, and he and Elisha are able to cross over on dry ground.

Suddenly a chariot of fire appears, drawn by horses of fire. In the chariot, Elijah is taken up by a whirlwind into heaven. Elisha calls out: 'My father, my father! I can see the chariot of Israel and its horsemen!' And then Elijah is gone.

G. Doré

The Children Destroyed by Bears

And he went up from thence unto Bethel: and as he was going up by the way, there came forth little children out of the city, and mocked him, and said unto him, Go up, thou bald head. And he turned back, and looked on them, and cursed them in the name of the Lord. And there came forth two she bears out of the wood, and tare forty and two children of them.

(2 Kings 2: 23–24)

While the prophet Elisha is on his way from Jericho to Bethel, some children make fun of him, shouting: 'Off you go, baldy!' Elisha curses them, and suddenly two she-bears appear out of the woods and tear forty-two of the children to pieces.

The Death of Jezebel

And he said, Throw her down. So they threw her down: and some of her blood was sprinkled on the wall, and on the horses: and he trode her under foot.

(2 Kings 9: 33)

Jezebel led her husband, King Ahab of Israel, and their sons to abandon the Lord and to worship her god, Baal. The prophet Elijah has prophesied that when Jezebel dies, she will not be buried but will instead be eaten by dogs.

Ahab is now dead, and his son Joram is king of Israel, but God has Jehu, an Israelite general, anointed king to replace him. Jehu leads a rebellion against Joram and, having killed him, goes to confront Jezebel in her palace.

Jehu orders Jezebel's servants to throw her out of the palace window, and she falls to her death. Her body is left lying where it has fallen, and when eventually servants are sent to bury it, there is nothing left but her head, her hands and her feet. Dogs have eaten the rest. And so Elijah's prophecy is fulfilled.

Amos

The words of Amos, who was among the herdmen of Tekoa, which he saw concerning Israel: The Lord will roar from Zion, and utter his voice from Jerusalem; and the habitations of the shepherds shall mourn, and the top of Carmel shall wither.

(Amos 1: 1–2)

Amos is a shepherd and fig-grower in Tekoa, to the south of Jerusalem, and therefore a citizen of the kingdom of Judah. But he is called by God to go to Bethel, one of the religious centres of the kingdom of Israel, to denounce the sins of the people of Israel and warn them that God's judgement on them is coming.

Isaiah

Also I heard the voice of the Lord, saying, Whom shall I send, and who will go for us? Then said I, Here am I; send me.

(Isaiah 6: 8)

The prophet Isaiah has a vision in which he sees God sitting on a high throne, with his robes filling the temple, and round him six-winged seraphim. The seraphim are praising God, and the temple is shaking with the sound of their voices.

Isaiah is dismayed at this vision, because he knows he is a sinful man, but he has seen God. However, one of the seraphim lifts a hot coal from the altar and touches Isaiah's lips with it, telling him that his sins are forgiven.

Then Isaiah hears the Lord calling: 'Who will be my messenger?', and he replies: 'I will. Send me.'

G. Doré

The Destruction of Leviathan

In that day the Lord with his sore and great and strong sword shall punish leviathan the piercing serpent, even leviathan that crooked serpent; and he shall slay the dragon that is in the sea.

(Isaiah 27:1)

The prophet Isaiah is prophesying about a coming day of judgement. On that day, God will kill the serpent Leviathan and the dragon of the sea. (These creatures represent nations that have been oppressing Israel.)

H. PISAN

Micah Exhorting the Israelites to Repentance

They build up Zion with blood, and Jerusalem with iniquity. The heads judge for reward, and the priests teach for hire, and the prophets divine for money. Therefore shall Zion be plowed as a field, and Jerusalem shall become heaps.

(MICAH 3: 10–12)

The prophet Micah denounces the corruption he sees in Jerusalem and Judah, where there is murder and injustice, and where the rulers, priests and prophets take money and bribes for their services.

Micah sets out clearly what God demands. It is not sacrifices he wants but virtue, morality and justice: 'What doth the Lord require of thee, but to do justly, and to love mercy, and to walk humbly with thy God?'

The Strange Nations Slain by the Lions of Samaria

The nations which thou hast removed, and placed in the cities of Samaria, know not the manner of the God of the land: therefore he hath sent lions among them, and, behold, they slay them, because they know not the manner of the God of the land.

(2 Kings 17: 26)

After a three-year siege of the city of Samaria, the Assyrians conquer Israel, and the Israelite people are deported to Assyria. To replace them, the Assyrian king brings in people from Babylon and other cities. However, these new inhabitants of Israel do not worship the Lord, and as a punishment God sends lions among them and many people are killed.

Jeremiah

And the Lord said unto me, Behold, I have put my words in thy mouth. See, I have this day set thee over the nations and over the kingdoms, to root out, and to pull down, and to destroy, and to throw down, to build, and to plant.

(Jeremiah 1: 9–10)

When Jeremiah is called to be a prophet, God tells him that he was chosen for this purpose even before he was born. Jeremiah protests that he is too young for the task, and does not know what to say, but God says that he will give him the words to say when the time comes. God warns Jeremiah that everyone in Judah – kings, officials, priests and people – will be against him, but he will be given the strength to stand up to them.

The People Mourning over the Ruins of Jerusalem

How doth the city sit solitary, that was full of people! How is she become as a widow! She that was great among the nations, how is she become tributary!

(LAMENTATIONS 1: 1)

Jerusalem, the capital city of the kingdom of Judah, is captured and destroyed by the Babylonians under King Nebuchadrezzar, and many of her citizens are deported to the east. The people mourn her greatness, which is now gone.

Ezekiel Prophesying

Now it came to pass, as I was among the captives by the river of Chebar, that the heavens were opened, and I saw visions of God. And he said unto me, Son of man, I send thee to the children of Israel, to a rebellious nation that hath rebelled against me: they and their fathers have transgressed against me, even unto this very day.

(EZEKIEL 1: 1; 2: 3)

Jerusalem has been captured and destroyed by the Babylonians and many of its people deported to the east. Ezekiel, a priest, is one of those now living in Babylonia, beside the River Chebar.

One day he has a vision of God. He sees a storm coming from the north and, in the middle of the storm, four living beings, each with four wings, four faces, four hands, and hooves. Above these living beings is a crystal dome, and above the dome a throne on which is sitting a figure resembling a man. Ezekiel hears a voice speaking to him, calling him to be a prophet.

Doré
C. LAPLANTE

The Vision of the Dry Bones

And he said unto me, Son of man, can these bones live? And I answered, O Lord God, thou knowest.

(EZEKIEL 37: 3)

In a prophecy he receives from God, Ezekiel is shown a valley covered with dry bones. God asks him whether the bones can live again, and Ezekiel replies that God alone can answer that question.

God tells Ezekiel to prophesy to the bones that he will put flesh on them and breathe life into them, and when Ezekiel does so, that is exactly what happens. God then explains to Ezekiel that Israel is like these dry bones, believing itself to be with no future and no hope, but that he will make the nation live again and return to Jerusalem.

Esther Accusing Haman

For we are sold, I and my people, to be destroyed, to be slain, and to perish. Then the king Ahasuerus answered and said unto Esther the queen, Who is he, and where is he, that durst presume in his heart to do so? And Esther said, The adversary and enemy is this wicked Haman. Then Haman was afraid before the king and the queen.

(Esther 7: 4–6)

Esther is the Jewish queen of King Ahasuerus (or Xerxes) of Persia. Haman, one of Ahasuerus' chief officials, angered by the refusal of Mordecai, Esther's adoptive father, to bow to him, is planning to kill every Jew in the Persian Empire.

Mordecai learns of the plot and asks for Esther's help to prevent it. At a banquet she has prepared for the king and Haman, Esther denounces Haman. And Haman is hanged on the gallows he had prepared for Mordecai.

Daniel

Then Arioch brought in Daniel before the king, and said unto him, I have found a man of the captives of Judah, that will make known unto the king the interpretation.

(Daniel: 2: 25)

After the fall of Jerusalem, many people are deported to Babylon, including four young men: Daniel, Hananiah, Mishael and Azariah. The Babylonians train them to be court officials, but from God they receive knowledge and wisdom, and Daniel is also given the ability to interpret dreams.

One night, King Nebuchadnezzar has a worrying dream. His wise men and astrologers are unable to tell him what his dream was and explain its meaning, which angers the king so much that he gives orders for all the wise men and astrologers in Babylon to be put to death, including Daniel and his companions.

God reveals to Daniel what Nebuchadnezzar's dream was, and what it meant. Daniel is taken to the king, and when he explains the dream to him, the king is so pleased that he makes Daniel chief of all the royal advisers, and governor of Babylon.

Shadrach, Meshach, and Abed-nego in the Fiery Furnace

Then Nebuchadnezzar the king was astonied, and rose up in haste, and spake, and said unto his counsellors, Did not we cast three men bound into the midst of the fire?

(Daniel 3: 24)

King Nebuchadnezzar of Babylon sets up a golden idol and gives orders that everyone must bow down and worship it. Three young Jewish men, Hananiah, Mishael and Azariah (also known by their Babylonian names of Shadrach, Meshach and Abed-nego), refuse to do so and as punishment are thrown into a blazing furnace.

But when Nebuchadnezzar looks into the furnace, he sees four men walking about in it. God has sent an angel to rescue Shadrach, Meshach and Abed-nego. When they step out of the furnace, the three young men have not so much as a scorch-mark on their clothing.

G.Doré

Daniel Interpreting the Writing on the Wall

In the same hour came forth fingers of a man's hand, and wrote over against the candlestick upon the plaister of the wall of the king's palace. And this is the writing that was written, MENE, MENE, TEKEL, UPHARSIN.

(Daniel 5: 5, 25)

Belshazzar, the son of Nebuchadnezzar, is now king of Babylonia. During a banquet, a human hand appears and writes something on the wall, but none of Belshazzar's wise men and astrologers can read the words.

Belshazzar's mother reminds him that Daniel, one of his court officials, was able to interpret a dream for Nebuchadnezzar. Daniel is sent for, and interprets the writing. He tells the king that this is the message God has for him: MENE, MENE, TEKEL, UPHARSIN. *Mene* means 'numbered': God has numbered the days of Belshazzar's kingdom and is bringing it to an end. *Tekel* means 'weighed': Belshazzar has been weighed in the balance and has not measured up. *Upharsin* means 'and divided': Belshazzar's kingdom will be divided between the Medes and the Persians.

That very night, Belshazzar is killed and Darius the Mede becomes king.

Daniel in the Den of Lions

My God hath sent his angel, and hath shut the lions' mouths, that they have not hurt me.

(Daniel 6: 22)

Daniel is such an efficient administrator that King Darius intends to make him the highest official in the land. Other officials, jealous of Daniel's success, decide to attack him through his faith. They persuade Darius to pass a decree that any person who offers prayers or petitions to anyone other than the king will be thrown into a den of lions. Daniel, however, continues to pray openly to God.

When Daniel's rivals denounce him to the king, Darius is forced to consent to Daniel being thrown to the lions. The next morning, after a sleepless night, Darius hurries to the lions' den, fearing the worst. But God has sent an angel to close the lions' mouths and Daniel is alive and unharmed. On Darius' orders, the officials who brought the accusation against Daniel are themselves thrown into the lions' den.

The Vision of the Four Beasts

Daniel spake and said, I saw in my vision by night, and, behold, the four winds of the heaven strove upon the great sea. And four great beasts came up from the sea, diverse one from another.

(Daniel 7: 2–3)

One night as Daniel is lying in his bed, he has a strange dream. He sees a storm over the sea, and out of the sea come four strange and terrifying creatures. The first is like a lion with eagle's wings; the second is like a bear, and it has three ribs between its teeth; the third is like a leopard with four heads and four wings; and the fourth is a beast with iron teeth, bronze claws and ten horns.

An angel explains to Daniel that these creatures represent four empires that are to arise on earth.

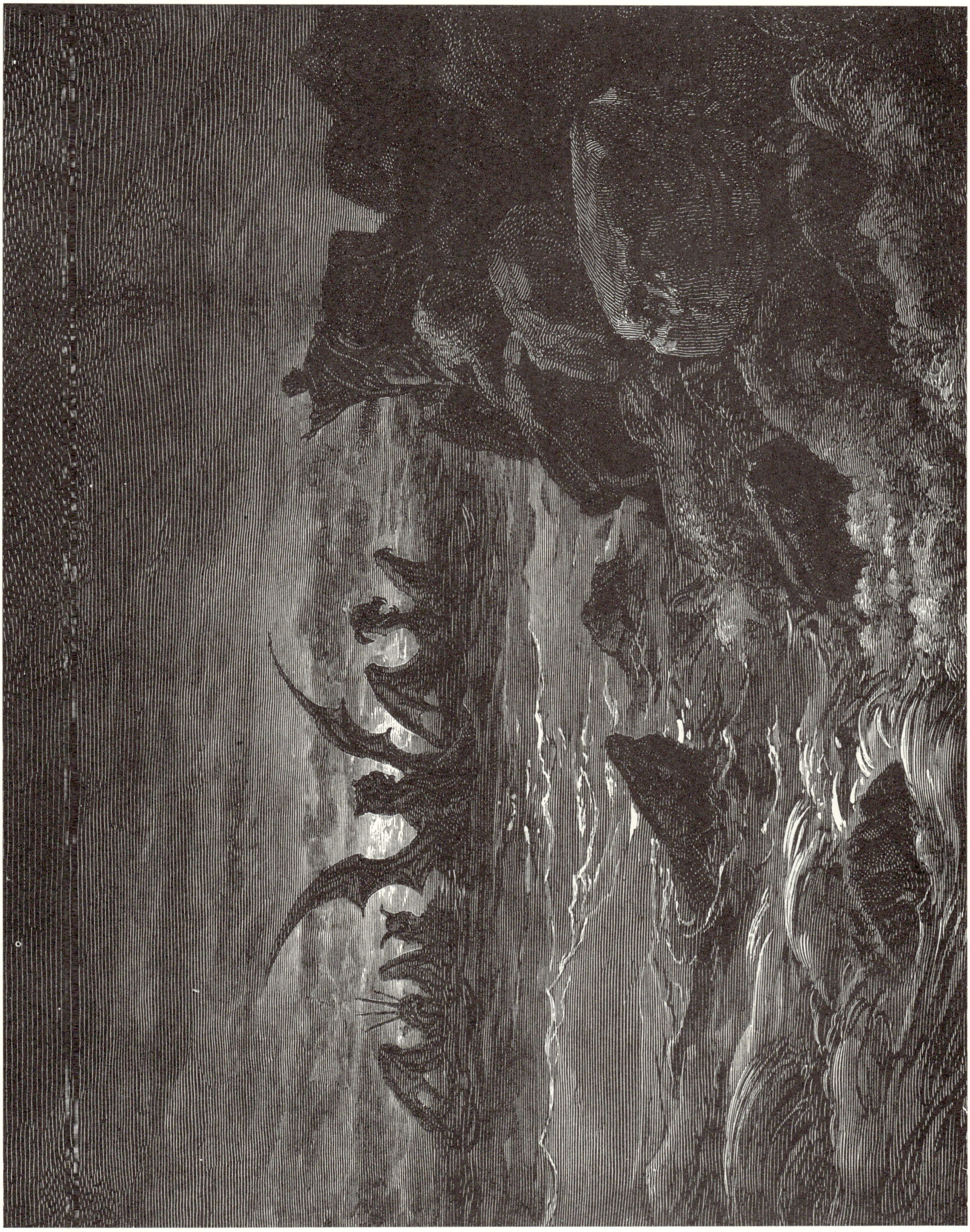

Cyrus Restoring the Vessels of the Temple

Cyrus the king brought forth the vessels of the house of the Lord, which Nebuchadnezzar had brought forth out of Jerusalem, and had put in the house of his gods, and numbered them unto Sheshbazzar, the prince of Judah.

(EZRA 1: 7–8)

The Persians have conquered Babylonia, and Cyrus is now king. God inspires Cyrus with the idea of rebuilding the temple in Jerusalem that was destroyed by the Babylonian king, Nebuchadnezzar. Cyrus decrees that the people of Judah are free to go back to Jerusalem to undertake the reconstruction.

Cyrus also brings out from the temple in Babylon the gold and silver dishes, and other utensils that Nebuchadnezzar looted from the temple in Jerusalem. There are more than five thousand dishes in all, and these Cyrus entrusts to Sheshbazzar to take back to Jerusalem.

G. Doré

The Rebuilding of the Temple

Many of the priests and Levites and chief of the fathers, who were ancient men, that had seen the first house, when the foundation of this house was laid before their eyes, wept with a loud voice; and many shouted aloud for joy.

(EZRA 3: 12)

About fifty years have passed since Jerusalem and its temple were destroyed and the people of Judah deported to Babylon. Babylon has been conquered by the Persians, and Cyrus, the Persian king, has instructed the Jews to return to Jerusalem and rebuild the temple.

Among those who set about the reconstruction are men who are old enough to remember the first temple before it was destroyed, and for them, seeing the foundations of the new temple being laid is an emotional experience.

Enemies hinder the reconstruction work but eventually the temple is rebuilt.

The Vision of the Four Chariots

And the angel answered and said unto me, These are the four spirits of the heavens, which go forth from standing before the Lord of all the earth.

(Zechariah 6: 5)

Prophesying at a time when the rebuilding of the temple in Jerusalem has temporarily been forbidden by the Persian king, Zechariah has a series of visions. In one vision, he sees four chariots coming out from between two bronze mountains. The first chariot is being pulled by red horses, the second by black horses, the third by white horses and the fourth by dappled-grey horses. The angel who is with Zechariah explains that in the chariots are four heavenly spirits, who are going out from the presence of God and travelling over the face of the earth as his agents.

Zechariah's prophecies encourage the Jews to press on with the reconstruction of the temple.

Artaxerxes Granting Liberty to the Jews

I make a decree, that all they of the people of Israel in my realm which are minded of their own freewill to go up to Jerusalem, go with thee.

(Ezra 7: 13)

Many years after the rebuilding of the temple in Jerusalem, Ezra, a priest and scholar who has a thorough knowledge of the Law, leaves Babylon and returns to Jerusalem. With him, by permission of the king, Artaxerxes, go many other Jews who want to return to their homeland.

Ezra Reading the Law in the Hearing of the People

And Ezra opened the book in the sight of all the people. And Ezra blessed the Lord, the great God. And all the people answered, Amen, Amen, with lifting up their hands: and they bowed their heads, and worshipped the Lord with their faces to the ground.

(Nehemiah 8: 5–6)

Ezra, a Jewish priest, has returned from Babylon to Jerusalem in order to teach the people the Law of Moses. All the people gather in Jerusalem to hear him. Everyone stands when Ezra opens the book of the Law; then, when Ezra praises the Lord, they all respond 'Amen, Amen', and bow down in worship.

Ezra reads the Law to the people from dawn till noon, and then it is explained to them so that they understand it.

Job Hearing of His Ruin

And said, Naked came I out of my mother's womb, and naked shall I return thither: the Lord gave, and the Lord hath taken away; blessed be the name of the Lord.

(Job 1: 21)

Job is a rich man, in fact the richest man in the land. He owns large flocks and herds, and has a large household of servants. He also has a large family.

Job is a God-fearing and pious man. However, when God points Job out to Satan as an example of a good man, Satan challenges God, saying that Job is only pious and God-fearing because God has given him so much. 'Take away all the Job has,' says Satan to the Lord, 'and he will curse you.'

God gives Satan permission to test Job, and Satan causes misfortune after misfortune to rain down on Job until he loses all he once had: his flocks and herds, his servants and his children. However, Job remains stoical, and does not sin by blaming God for his misfortunes.

Job and His Friends

Wherefore then hast thou brought me forth out of the womb? Oh that I had given up the ghost, and no eye had seen me! I should have been as though I had not been; I should have been carried from the womb to the grave.

(Job 10: 18–19)

Job is a pious and God-fearing man who has met with great misfortune, because Satan is trying to prove to God that Job is pious and good only because God had granted him great wealth and a large family.

Job has now lost family, wealth and health. Three friends come to comfort him, but only make matters worse by trying to persuade Job that since God rewards good and punishes evil, he must have done something really bad to have merited these disasters.

Eventually, Job's spirit breaks and he curses the day he was born, wishing he had died at birth.

Jonah Cast forth by the Whale

And the Lord spake unto the fish, and it vomited out Jonah upon the dry land.

(Jonah 2: 10)

God tells Jonah, a prophet, to go to Nineveh, a city of great wickedness. Jonah, however, does not want to do this, and instead boards a ship that will take him far away from Nineveh. During the voyage, God causes a storm to blow up and, realizing that he is to blame, Jonah tells the crew to throw him overboard.

At God's command, a huge fish swallows Jonah, and he spends three days and nights in the fish's stomach. Then God tells the fish to disgorge Jonah onto dry land.

Doré
Jonnard

Jonah Preaching to the Ninevites

So Jonah arose, and went unto Nineveh, and he cried, and said, Yet forty days, and Nineveh shall be overthrown.

(Jonah 3: 3–4)

Jonah has been told by God to go to Nineveh to warn its people to mend their ways. Trying to escape this responsibility, Jonah attempts to flee by boat, but a storm arises and Jonah is thrown overboard. A huge fish swallows him and then spits him out again safely onto dry land.

God again tells Jonah to go to Nineveh, and this time he obeys. Warned by Jonah that God intends to destroy the city in forty days' time because of its wickedness, the citizens of Nineveh repent. God therefore spares the city.

The Apocrypha

The Apocrypha are religious writings not found in the Hebrew version of the Jewish scriptures, but included in the Septuagint, the Greek translation of these scriptures, produced in Egypt during the 3rd and 2nd centuries BC for the use of Greek-speaking Jews.

The status of the Apocrypha within the Jewish and Christian communities has varied over the past 2,000 years. They were definitively rejected from the canon of Jewish scripture in the 1st century AD, but were generally accepted by the early Christian church until St Jerome, in the late 4th century, excluded them from his definitive list of the books of the Old and New Testaments. Nevertheless, they remain part of the canon of the Roman Catholic Church and the Orthodox churches. Their status within Protestantism varies from denomination to denomination, and they are included in some Protestant versions of the Bible but excluded from others.

Of the writings generally included in the Apocrypha, seven are represented in the present book: Tobit, Judith, Additions to the Book of Esther, Susanna, Bel and the Dragon (these last two being additions to the Book of Daniel), and 1st and 2nd Maccabees. Only the last two are truly historical works, both recounting the events of the Jewish revolt against the Seleucid kings during the 2nd century BC. The other books, regardless of their historical settings, are not written as books of history but rather to convey an ethical or religious message.

Finally, the illustration of 'Susanna in the Bath' (see p. 209) needs a brief comment. As can be seen from Doré's signature in the bottom right-hand corner, the illustration has been printed in reverse. This is not an error: this plate was printed in reverse in the original French and English editions of the Bible.

Tobias and the Angel

The angel said, Open the fish, and take the heart and the liver and the gall, and put them up safely. So the young man did as the angel commanded him; and when they had roasted the fish, they did eat it.

(Tobit 6: 4–5)

Tobit is a poor Israelite living in Nineveh in Assyria, who has been blinded in an unfortunate accident. One day he remembers that he once left some money with a relative in the town of Rages in Persia, and he sends his son Tobias to get it. Tobias travels with a companion, Azarias, who, unknown to Tobit and his family, is in fact the angel Raphael.

Eventually, Tobias and Azarias come to the River Tigris. As Tobias steps into the river to wash, a huge fish leaps at him. Azarias tells Tobias to catch the fish, and to remove and keep its heart, liver and gall. When Tobias asks Azarias the reason for this, the angel explains that smoke created by burning the heart and liver will drive away evil spirits and demons, and that the gall will cure blindness.

The Angel Raphael and the Family of Tobit

I am Raphael, one of the seven holy angels. By the will of our God I came. Now therefore give God thanks: for I go up to him that sent me.

(TOBIT 12: 15, 18, 20)

Tobias, the son of Tobit, a poor, blind Israelite living in Nineveh, journeys to Persia for some money that Tobit once left with a relative. Tobias is accompanied on his journey by Azarias, who is in fact the angel Raphael. Along the way, Tobias catches a fish and, on Azarias' advice, removes its heart and liver, which can be used to drive away demons, and its gall, which can cure blindness.

Stopping en route at the house of Raguel, Tobias uses the fish's heart and liver to drive away the demon, Asmodeus, who has been tormenting Raguel's daughter, Sara. Tobias then marries Sara; Azarias fetches the money from Tobit's relative; Tobias, Sara and Azarias return to Nineveh; and Tobias uses the gall to cure Tobit's blindness.

Azarias then reveals his true identity, and explains that he was sent to them by God, to whom he is now returning.

Judith and Holofernes

Then she came to the pillar of the bed, which was at Holofernes' head, and took down his fauchion from thence, and approached to his bed, and took hold of the hair of his head, and said, Strengthen me, O Lord God of Israel, this day. And she smote twice upon his neck with all her might, and she took away his head from him.

(JUDITH 13: 6–8)

Holofernes is the general of an Assyrian army that is invading Judah. In order to capture the strategic town of Bethulia, Holofernes has cut off its water supply. When the town's water runs out, the people prepare to surrender to the Assyrians. However, they are persuaded to hold on for five more days in the hope that God will rescue them.

Judith, a pious and beautiful widow living in Bethulia, goes to Holofernes on the pretext of telling him how he can defeat the people of Judah. After an intimate meal with Judith, Holofernes falls into a drunken sleep. Judith takes his sword, cuts off his head and takes it back to Bethulia. This heartens the Jews, who then attack the Assyrians. The Assyrians, finding their general dead, flee in fear and confusion.

Esther before the King

And upon the third day, she stood before the king, who sat upon his royal throne; and he was very dreadful. Then lifting up his countenance, he looked very fiercely upon her: and the queen fell down, and was pale, and fainted. Then God changed the spirit of the king into mildness, who in a fear leaped from his throne, and took her in his arms, till she came to herself again, and comforted her with loving words.

(ESTHER 15: 1, 6–8)

Esther is the Jewish queen of the king of Persia, who has been persuaded to pass a decree ordering the murder of every Jew in the Persian Empire.

After three days of prayer and fasting, Esther goes to her husband to plead for her people. Although outwardly cheerful, inwardly she is 'in anguish for fear', knowing that the Jews are out of favour with the king. And when she sees the king on his throne, glowering at her fiercely, she faints.

At this, the king's mood immediately changes. He jumps down from his throne, takes Esther in his arms, and comforts her, reassuring her that she at least will not be killed.

Susanna in the Bath

The two elders rose up, and ran unto her, saying, Behold, the garden doors are shut, that no man can see us, and we are in love with thee; therefore consent unto us, and lie with us. If thou wilt not, we will bear witness against thee, that a young man was with thee.

(Susanna 19-21)

Susanna is a beautiful and devout young woman, the wife of a wealthy Jew living in Babylon.

One hot day she goes out into her garden to bathe. Two elderly judges, who have become inflamed with desire for her, are already hiding there, hoping to catch sight of her. When Susanna sends her maids back into the house, the two men come out from where they have been hiding and offer her a terrible choice: she must allow them to have their way with her, or else they will say that they found her with a lover. Susanna absolutely refuses to commit the sin they are demanding of her.

The next day, she is brought to trial, and the two judges tell the story they have concocted. Being respected members of the community, they are of course believed, and Susanna is condemned to be stoned to death.

The Justification of Susanna

And they arose against the two elders, for Daniel had convicted them of false witness by their own mouth: And according to the law of Moses they did unto them in such sort as they maliciously intended to do to their neighbour: and they put them to death.

(SUSANNA 61–62)

Susanna is a beautiful and devout young Jewish woman who has been condemned to death for adultery on the basis of a story maliciously fabricated by two elderly judges, angry at her refusal to make love to them.

As she is led away to be stoned to death, she cries out to God, reminding him of her innocence. In answer to her prayer, God moves Daniel to speak up on her behalf. He tells the crowd that the judges are lying and that he can prove it. Separating the two old men, Daniel questions each in turn, and finds a crucial discrepancy in their stories, so proving that they were lying. The two judges then suffer the punishment they had intended to see inflicted on Susanna.

Daniel Confounding the Priests of Bel

Then said the king unto him, Thinkest thou not that Bel is a living god? seest thou not how much he eateth and drinketh every day? Then Daniel smiled, and said, O king, be not deceived: for this is but clay within, and brass without, and did never eat or drink any thing.

(Bel and the Dragon 6–7)

Daniel is a young Jewish man living in Babylon, where the people worship the god Bel. When Daniel is asked by the Babylonian king why he does not worship Bel, Daniel replies that Bel is only an idol, not the true and living God. When the king points out that, since Bel consumes the offerings that are brought to him each day, he too must be a living god, Daniel undertakes to prove that this is not the case.

Food and wine are set before the idol, but when the priests leave, Daniel has ashes scattered over the floor of the temple. The next morning, the offerings are gone, but there are footprints in the ashes, showing that the priests have secretly entered the temple during the night and eaten and drunk the offerings. The king has the priests executed and allows Daniel to destroy the idol.

The Courage of a Mother

It came to pass also, that seven brethren with their mother were taken, and compelled by the king against the law to taste swine's flesh, and were tormented with scourges and whips.

The mother was marvellous above all, and worthy of honourable memory: for when she saw her seven sons slain within the space of one day, she bare it with a good courage, because of the hope that she had in the Lord.

Last of all after the sons the mother died.

(2 MACCABEES 7: 1, 20, 41)

King Antiochus is determined to promote Greek customs and culture throughout his kingdom, which includes Judaea. A statue of the Greek god Zeus is erected in the Jewish temple, and the Jews are forbidden to worship God. All Jewish practices are banned.

Among the things forbidden to Jews by the Law of Moses is the eating of pork, but by torture and the threat of death the king tries to persuade seven brothers and their mother to eat some. One by one, in the sight of their mother, the brothers are tortured to death, resolutely refusing to break God's law.

Not only does the mother courageously bear the sight of her sons being tortured and killed, she herself exhorts them to hold steadfastly to the Law. And finally, she too is killed for her faith.

The Angel Sent to Deliver Israel

And as they were at Jerusalem, there appeared before them on horseback one in white clothing, shaking his armour of gold.

(2 MACCABEES 11: 8)

The attempts by King Antiochus to impose Greek customs and religion on the Jews and to forbid the Jews to follow their own religion has caused a Jewish revolt under the leadership of Judas Maccabeus.

When the king's forces invade Judaea and besiege the town of Beth-zur, the Jews pray to the Lord to send them an angel to help them. Before the battle between the Maccabean forces and the army of the king, an angel appears to the Jewish army, riding on horseback and wearing gold armour. Encouraged by this sign, the Maccabeans win the day and put their enemies to flight.

The Death of Eleazar

Eleazar, perceiving that one of the beasts, armed with royal harness, was higher than all the rest, and supposing that the king was upon him, ran courageously through the midst of the battle, slaying on the right hand and on the left. Which done, he crept under the elephant, and thrust him under, and slew him: whereupon the elephant fell down upon him, and there he died.

(1 Maccabees 6: 43–46)

During the Jewish revolt against the Syrian king, led by Judas Maccabeus, there is a battle between the king's forces and the Maccabean army at the town of Beth-zur.

During the battle, Judas' brother Eleazar notices that one of the enemy's battle-elephants is taller than the others and is equipped with royal armour. Supposing the king himself to be on the elephant, Eleazar courageously fights his way through the enemy troops until he gets beneath it, whereupon he stabs and kills it. The dying elephant, however, falls on top of Eleazar, and he too dies.

The New Testament

The New Testament tells the story of the birth, life, death and resurrection of Jesus, and of the establishment and growth of the Christian church.

The story of Jesus is told in the four gospels, written by Matthew, Mark, Luke and John. Luke continues his story in the Acts of the Apostles, recounting the formation and expansion of the church, and especially St Paul's missionary journeys and his journey to Rome. The books following Acts contain letters written by Paul and others to people, to churches, or to the early church in general. The last book of the Bible is the Revelation of St John the Divine, in which John describes a series of visions he has, culminating in a vision of a new heaven, a new earth and a new Jerusalem.

The New Testament illustrations are in historical rather than Biblical order. The illustrations depicting the gospel story are, therefore, ordered as far as possible in chronological order – 'as far as possible' being the most that is possible, since the gospels themselves differ with regard to the inclusion and ordering of key events. And although the illustrative Bible quotations are always taken from one gospel, the accompanying commentaries may contain elements from more than one.

The illustration on p. 255 requires two comments. Firstly, it is the only illustration in this book that is allegorical rather than descriptive. And secondly, although the illustration title reflects a belief long held by the church, there is no reason to believe that the prostitute was Mary Magdalene, nor indeed that Mary Magdalene was ever a prostitute.

The Annunciation

And the angel said unto her, Fear not, Mary: for thou hast found favour with God. And, behold, thou shalt conceive in thy womb, and bring forth a son, and shalt call his name JESUS.

(LUKE 1: 30–31)

Mary is a Jewish girl, living in Nazareth and engaged to be married to Joseph. One day the angel Gabriel comes to her and tells her that, although unmarried, she will, through the power of the Holy Spirit, conceive and bear a son, whom she will name Jesus. Jesus will be a great king, and his kingdom will last forever. He will be called the Son of the Highest and the Son of God.

In faith, Mary accepts the role that God has chosen for her: 'Behold the handmaid of the Lord; be it unto me according to thy word.'

The Nativity

And there were shepherds abiding in the field, keeping watch over their flock by night. And the angel said unto them, I bring you good tidings of great joy. For unto you is born this day in the city of David a Saviour, which is Christ the Lord. Ye shall find the babe wrapped in swaddling clothes, lying in a manger. And the shepherds said one to another, Let us now go even unto Bethlehem, and see this thing which is come to pass.

(Luke 2: 8, 10–12, 15)

About the time when Mary is due to give birth, she and Joseph have to leave Nazareth and travel to Bethlehem to be registered in a census. Since there is no room for them in the inn, they have to spend the night in a stable, and there Mary gives birth to Jesus. She uses the animals' manger as a cot for her baby.

Not far away, there are some shepherds out in the fields with their flocks. An angel appears to them and tells them that the Saviour has been born in Bethlehem, and that they will find him lying in a manger.

The shepherds hurry at once to Bethlehem, and, just as the angel had said, they find Mary and Joseph in a stable and Jesus lying in the manger.

The Wise Men Guided by the Star

There came wise men from the east to Jerusalem, saying, Where is he that is born King of the Jews? for we have seen his star in the east, and are come to worship him. And, lo, the star went before them, till it came and stood over where the young child was.

(MATTHEW 2: 1–2, 9)

Some Persian astrologers, seeing a strange star in the sky and recognizing that it marks the birth of a great king, travel to Judaea to search for him.

First they come to Jerusalem, and ask where the baby is to be found. On learning that Scripture prophecy says that he will be born in Bethlehem, they set off again, following the star until it stops above the very house where Jesus and his parents are now living.

The astrologers enter the house, and seeing Jesus, they kneel down and worship him, presenting to him their gifts of gold, frankincense and myrrh.

The Flight into Egypt

Behold, the angel of the Lord appeareth to Joseph in a dream, saying, Arise, and take the young child and his mother, and flee into Egypt, and be thou there until I bring thee word: for Herod will seek the young child to destroy him.

(Matthew 2: 13)

Frightened by the news of the birth of a new king, Herod asks the Persian astrologers to come back once they have found Jesus and tell him where the baby is, pretending that he too wants to go to worship him. However, God warns them in a dream not to go back to Herod.

After the astrologers leave, God sends an angel to Joseph to warn him to flee into Egypt with Mary and Jesus, because Herod will certainly try to kill the child. Joseph, Mary and Jesus remain in Egypt until Herod is dead.

The Massacre of the Innocents

Then Herod sent forth, and slew all the children that were in Bethlehem, and in all the coasts thereof, from two years old and under.

(MATTHEW 2: 16)

When King Herod learns that the astrologers have left the country without telling him where he can find Jesus, he is furious. Unable to identify Jesus, the new king he is so afraid of, he gives orders that all boys in the Bethlehem area, aged two years or less, are to be killed.

Jesus with the Doctors

After three days they found him in the temple, sitting in the midst of the doctors, both hearing them, and asking them questions. And all that heard him were astonished at his understanding and answers.

(LUKE 2: 46–47)

When Jesus is twelve years old, he and his parents go to Jerusalem to celebrate the Passover. On their way back home, Mary and Joseph discover that Jesus is not in fact travelling with them and the other members of their party. He must still be in Jerusalem. So they turn back to search for him.

They search for three days, and at last find Jesus in the Temple, sitting with the Jewish teachers, listening to them and asking them questions. Everyone who hears him is amazed at the wisdom and understanding of this twelve-year-old boy.

When Mary asks Jesus how he could be so thoughtless as to leave them without telling them where he was, Jesus says that they should have known that they would find him in the Temple, his Father's house.

John the Baptist Preaching in the Wilderness

John did baptize in the wilderness, and preach the baptism of repentance for the remission of sins. And there went out unto him all the land of Judaea, and they of Jerusalem, and were all baptized of him in the river of Jordan, confessing their sins.

(MARK 1: 4–5)

John the Baptist is the son of Elizabeth, a relative of Mary, the mother of Jesus. He lives and preaches in the desert, wears clothes of camel hair, and eats locusts and wild honey.

In his preaching, John calls on the people to repent of their sins and be baptized, because the Kingdom of Heaven is fast approaching. Crowds come from Jerusalem and all over Judaea to be baptized by him in the River Jordan.

Some people wonder whether John might be the promised Messiah, but he tells them that he only baptizes with water, while the one who is coming will baptize with the Holy Spirit.

The Baptism of Jesus

And Jesus, when he was baptized, went up straightway out of the water: and, lo, the heavens were opened unto him, and he saw the Spirit of God descending like a dove, and lighting upon him: And lo a voice from heaven, saying, This is my beloved Son, in whom I am well pleased.

(MATTHEW 3: 16–17)

John the Baptist lives and preaches in the desert, calling on people to repent and seek God's forgiveness for their sins. Crowds flock to him to be baptized in the River Jordan.

One day Jesus comes to be baptized by John. At first John refuses, saying that it is Jesus who should baptize him. Jesus, however, insists, and John consents. When Jesus comes out of the river after his baptism, he sees heaven opening and the Spirit of God coming down to him like a dove, and a voice is heard, saying: 'This is my beloved son, with whom I am very pleased.'

The Temptation of Jesus

And Jesus being full of the Holy Ghost returned from Jordan, and was led by the Spirit into the wilderness, being forty days tempted of the devil. And when the devil had ended all the temptation, he departed from him.

(LUKE 4: 1–2, 13)

After his baptism, Jesus goes out into the desert, where he stays for forty days. Satan tries to tempt Jesus, hungry after forty days of fasting, into misusing his powers by turning a stone into bread. This Jesus refuses to do.

Satan then takes Jesus to Jerusalem and challenges him to prove that he is the Son of God by throwing himself from the highest point on the Temple in the expectation that God will send angels to save him. This too, Jesus refuses to do.

Finally Satan promises that if Jesus worships him, he will be given power over all the kingdoms on earth. Again Jesus rejects Satan. And having thus failed to tempt Jesus into sin, Satan departs.

The Marriage in Cana

Jesus saith unto them, Fill the waterpots with water. And they filled them up to the brim. And he saith unto them, Draw out now, and bear unto the governor of the feast.

(John 2: 7–8)

Jesus, his mother and his disciples are attending a wedding celebration in Cana. The wine runs out, and Jesus is persuaded by his mother to perform his first miracle. He tells the servants to fill their water jars with water, which they do. He then tells them to draw some of the water out of the jars again and to take it to the man in charge of the celebrations. When they do, they find that the water has turned into wine.

Jesus and the Woman of Samaria

There cometh a woman of Samaria to draw water: Jesus saith unto her, Give me to drink. Then saith the woman of Samaria unto him, How is it that thou, being a Jew, askest drink of me, which am a woman of Samaria? for the Jews have no dealings with the Samaritans.

(John 4: 7, 9)

On his way north from Judaea to Galilee, Jesus passes through Samaria. At the town of Sychar, he stops to rest at a well. When a Samaritan woman comes to the well to draw water, Jesus asks her for a drink, which surprises her because Jews generally will have nothing to do with Samaritans. Jesus tells that woman that if only she knew who she is speaking to, she would ask *him* for water, and he would give her the 'living water' that brings everlasting life.

When Jesus goes on to tell the woman about the five husbands that she has had, and that the man she is living with now is not her husband, she recognizes that he is a prophet, and wonders whether he might even be the Messiah.

Christ in the Synagogue

And he came to Nazareth, where he had been brought up: and, as his custom was, he went into the synagogue on the sabbath day, and stood up for to read.

(Luke 4: 16)

Jesus begins to preach in the synagogues in Galilee, and amazes everyone with his teaching. One Sabbath day, in the synagogue in Nazareth, Jesus reads a passage from the prophet Isaiah, and tells the congregation that the prophecy has been fulfilled that very day, as he read to them. Everyone is very impressed by Jesus' teaching, but they are also quite amazed, because the man is known to them as the son of Joseph, the local carpenter.

Jesus points out to them that prophets are never accepted by their own people, and quotes two stories from Scripture in which God shows greater kindness to Gentiles than he does to Israelites. This infuriates the people in the synagogue and they drag him to the top of a hill, intending to throw him off. But Jesus simply walks through the crowd and makes his way to Capernaum.

Jesus Healing the Man Possessed with a Devil

And they were all amazed, and spake among themselves, saying, What a word is this! for with authority and power he commandeth the unclean spirits, and they come out.

(LUKE 4: 36)

One Sabbath day, Jesus is teaching in the synagogue in Capernaum when a man possessed by a demon starts shouting at him. 'Go away! Leave us alone!' he shouts. 'I know who you are. You're the Holy One whom God has sent.'

Jesus tells the demon to be quiet and to come out of the man. The demon throws the man to the ground and leaves him, without doing him any further harm. Everyone is amazed at Jesus' power and authority, that even demons obey him.

Jesus Preaching at the Sea of Galilee

And he entered into one of the ships, which was Simon's, and prayed him that he would thrust out a little from the land. And he sat down, and taught the people out of the ship.

(LUKE 5: 3)

One day as Jesus is preaching to a large crowd by the edge of the Sea of Galilee, the people press closer and closer to him to hear what he is saying. Noticing two fishing boats pulled up onto the beach, he gets into one of them and asks Simon, the owner of the boat, to push it out into the water. Then he sits down in the boat and teaches the people from there.

The Sermon on the Mount

And seeing the multitudes, he went up into a mountain: and when he was set, his disciples came unto him: And he opened his mouth, and taught them.

(MATTHEW 5: 1–2)

Jesus journeys all over Galilee, teaching in the synagogues, preaching the good news about the Kingdom of God, and healing people who are ill or possessed by demons. Crowds gather to hear him; there are people from Galilee, from the region of the Ten Towns, from Jerusalem, from all over Judaea, and even from the other side of the River Jordan.

When Jesus sees the crowds, he goes up onto a hill and sits down, and his disciples gather round him. Then he teaches the people. Everyone is amazed at what he says, because Jesus speaks with real authority, not like the teachers of the Law whom they are used to listening to.

The Disciples Plucking Corn on the Sabbath

And it came to pass, that he went through the corn fields on the sabbath day; and his disciples began, as they went, to pluck the ears of corn.

(MARK 2: 23)

One Sabbath day, Jesus and his disciples are walking through a cornfield. Feeling hungry, the disciples pick some ears of corn and eat them. Some Pharisees see this and criticize them, because harvesting corn on the Sabbath is forbidden by Jewish religious law.

Jesus takes this opportunity to explain to the Pharisees that they have misunderstood the point of the Sabbath. The laws forbidding work on the Sabbath are intended by God to be a blessing, not a burden: 'The sabbath was made for man, and not man for the sabbath.'

G. Doré
PANNEMAKER - DOMS

Mary Magdalene Repentant

Her sins, which are many, are forgiven; for she loved much.

(Luke 7: 47)

Simon, a Pharisee, invites Jesus to eat with him. During the meal, a prostitute comes into the house and stands behind Jesus, weeping. She washes Jesus' feet with her tears and dries them with her hair, she kisses them, and then she pours perfume over them.

Simon is appalled at this, thinking that Jesus does not know the sort of woman she is. Jesus points out that the woman has done what Simon, his host, has not done: he did not give Jesus water to wash his feet, but the woman has washed his feet with her tears; he did not greet Jesus with a kiss, but she has not stopped kissing his feet; he did not give Jesus oil for his hair, but she has poured perfume over his feet. Jesus then says that the woman's sins have been forgiven because of her love and faith.

The Dumb Man Possessed

And he was casting out a devil, and it was dumb. And it came to pass, when the devil was gone out, the dumb spake; and the people wondered. But some of them said, He casteth out devils through Beelzebub the chief of the devils.

(LUKE 11: 14–15)

A man is brought to Jesus. He cannot speak because he is possessed by an evil spirit. When Jesus drives out the evil spirit, the man regains the power of speech.

The crowd who see this miracle are amazed, and begin to wonder whether Jesus might be the Messiah, but the Pharisees claim that Jesus' power to drive out evil spirits comes from the Prince of Demons himself. Jesus points out that the Pharisees' own followers prove that this is not so, because they too drive out evil spirits. It is by God's power that the evil spirits are driven out, and this shows that the Kingdom of God is already present.

Jesus Stilling the Tempest

And he arose, and rebuked the wind, and said unto the sea, Peace, be still. And the wind ceased, and there was a great calm.

(Mark 4: 39)

Jesus has been teaching crowds of people beside the Sea of Galilee. When the crowds leave, Jesus, the disciples, and others set off across the lake in small boats. Jesus falls asleep in the boat he is in.

Suddenly a storm blows up and the boats are buffeted by the wind and waves. Terrified, the disciples wake Jesus, saying: 'Master, does it not matter to you that we are all going to die?' Jesus stands up and commands the wind to stop and the sea to be still. And at once the wind dies down and the sea becomes calm.

G. Doré

Jesus Raising Up the Daughter of Jairus

And he took her by the hand, and called, saying, Maid, arise. And her spirit came again, and she arose straightway.

(Luke 8: 54–55)

One day Jesus is approached by Jairus, a leader in the local synagogue. Jairus begs Jesus to go with him and heal his twelve-year-old daughter, who is dying. Sadly, before Jesus can go with Jairus, a messenger comes from Jairus' house to say that the girl is dead. However, Jesus reassures Jairus, saying that if he only has faith, his daughter will get well again.

At Jairus' house, Jesus tells the mourners to stop weeping, because the girl is not dead, just sleeping. Everyone laughs at him, because they know the girl has died. But Jesus takes her hand and says to her: 'Little girl, get up.' And immediately life returns to her and she stands up.

The Daughter of Herod Receiving the Head of John the Baptist

But when Herod's birthday was kept, the daughter of Herodias danced before them, and pleased Herod. Whereupon he promised with an oath to give her whatsoever she would ask. And she, being before instructed of her mother, said, Give me here John Baptist's head in a charger.

(Matthew 14: 6–8)

John the Baptist has told Herod, the ruler of Galilee, that it was wrong for him to have married his brother's wife Herodias. For this, Herod has had John imprisoned.

On Herod's birthday, Herodias' daughter Salome dances for him. Herod is so delighted by her dancing that he promises her anything she asks for. Put up to it by her mother, she asks for the head of John the Baptist on a plate. Herod does not want to kill John, but having made the promise in front of so many people he has no choice. John is beheaded, and his head is brought to Salome, who takes it to her mother.

Christ Feeding the Multitude

And he commanded the multitude to sit down on the grass, and took the five loaves, and the two fishes, and looking up to heaven, he blessed, and brake, and gave the loaves to his disciples, and the disciples to the multitude. And they did all eat, and were filled.

(MATTHEW 14: 19–20)

Jesus has gone to a lonely place to be by himself, but the crowds have followed him and he has spent the day healing the sick. When evening comes, the disciples go to Jesus and suggest that since it is getting late, he should send everyone away to the nearest villages to buy food. But Jesus tells them that no one needs to buy food, and that the disciples themselves will feed them. The disciples are amazed at this, as all they have to offer is five loaves and two fish.

Jesus takes the loaves and the fish and blesses them. Then he breaks them up for the disciples to distribute to the crowd. Not only does everyone have enough to eat (and there are five thousand men in the crowd, not to mention women and children), after everyone has finished eating the disciples pick up twelve baskets of leftovers.

Jesus Walking on the Sea

So when they had rowed about five and twenty or thirty furlongs, they see Jesus walking on the sea, and drawing nigh unto the ship: and they were afraid.

(John 6: 19)

After Jesus has fed the crowd with only five loaves and two fish, and the people have all gone away, the disciples set off in a boat across the Sea of Galilee. Jesus does not go with them.

Darkness falls, and a storm blows up, causing rough seas. Suddenly, the disciples see Jesus coming across the water towards them. They are terrified, thinking it is a ghost, but Jesus reassures them, telling them not to be afraid because it really is him.

Peter starts to walk across the water towards Jesus, but in the strong wind he loses his nerve and starts to sink, calling to Jesus to save him. Jesus catches hold of him, chiding him for his lack of faith, and they both get into the boat. The wind dies down, and in no time at all they reach the opposite shore.

Jesus Healing the Sick

And great multitudes came unto him, having with them those that were lame, blind, dumb, maimed, and many others, and cast them down at Jesus' feet; and he healed them.

(MATTHEW 15: 30)

Jesus climbs a hill close to the Sea of Galilee, and as usual a large crowd gathers, bringing people to him who are lame, blind, crippled, unable to speak, or suffering from some other illness or disability. And Jesus heals them all. When the crowd see this, they praise God.

The Transfiguration

And after six days Jesus taketh with him Peter, and James, and John, and leadeth them up into an high mountain apart by themselves: and he was transfigured before them. And his raiment became shining, exceeding white as snow.

(Mark 9: 2–3)

Jesus takes the disciples Peter, James and John with him up a mountain where they can be alone, and there a change comes over him: his clothes turn a shining white. Then Elijah and Moses appear, and the three disciples see them talking to Jesus. They are so frightened, they are almost speechless. Peter offers to build shelters for Jesus, Moses and Elijah – it's the only thing he can think of to say.

A cloud appears and overshadows them, and they hear a voice from the cloud saying: 'This is my beloved Son: listen to him.' And then suddenly, when they look around, there is no one else there, just Jesus and themselves. Jesus tells them not to tell anyone else what they have seen until he has risen from the dead.

Jesus Healing the Lunatic

There came to him a certain man, kneeling down to him, and saying, Lord, have mercy on my son: for he is lunatick, and sore vexed: for ofttimes he falleth into the fire, and oft into the water.

(MATTHEW 17: 14–15)

One day a man approaches Jesus and asks him to take pity on his son, who has terrible seizures and often falls into fires or into water. He has already asked Jesus' disciples to help the boy, but they were not able to heal him. The man's son is brought to Jesus, and at his command the demon that is causing the seizures leaves the boy, and at that very moment he is cured.

G. Doré
CHAPON sc.

The Good Samaritan

A certain man went down from Jerusalem to Jericho, and fell among thieves, which stripped him of his raiment, and wounded him, and departed, leaving him half dead. But a certain Samaritan, as he journeyed, came where he was: and when he saw him, he had compassion on him.

(LUKE 10: 30, 33)

A teacher of the Law, discussing with Jesus what it means to 'love your neighbour as you love yourself', asks him who his 'neighbour' is. In reply, Jesus tells this story of the Good Samaritan:

'There was once a man who was attacked by robbers on his way from Jerusalem to Jericho. They stripped him of his clothes, beat him up, and left him for dead at the side of the road. A priest came by, but walked past on the other side of the road. A Levite, an assistant priest, went over to look at the man, and then walked on. However, just then a Samaritan came along. He took pity on the man, bound up his wounds, put him on his horse and took him to an inn.'

Arrival of the Good Samaritan at the Inn

He set him on his own beast, and brought him to an inn, and took care of him.

(Luke 10: 33)

In the story that Jesus is telling, a Samaritan comes across a Jew who has been robbed, beaten and left for dead. Jesus continues:

'The Samaritan took the injured man to an inn and looked after him. The next day, before he left, he gave the innkeeper two silver coins and asked him to take care of the man, promising that he would repay the innkeeper for any further expenses when he came back that way again.'

Jesus at the House of Martha and Mary

He entered into a certain village: and a certain woman named Martha received him into her house. And she had a sister called Mary.

(Luke 10: 38–39)

Jesus and his disciples come to the village of Bethany, where a woman whose name is Martha welcomes Jesus into her house. Martha has a sister, Mary.

Having Jesus as a guest, Martha busies herself around the house. Mary, on the other hand, sits beside Jesus to listen to what he has to say. Martha is annoyed about this, and asks him to tell Mary to come and help her. Jesus, however, tells Martha that she is fussing too much about things that do not really matter, and that by listening to him it is Mary who has chosen to do what is really important.

G. Doré
PANNEMAKER-DOMS

Jesus Preaching to the Multitude

There were gathered together an innumerable multitude of people, insomuch that they trode one upon another.

(LUKE 12: 1)

A huge crowd gathers to hear Jesus. They crowd round so tightly that they even stand on one another's feet!

While Jesus is talking, a man calls out to him from the crowd: 'Teacher, tell my brother to give me my fair share of what we have inherited.' Jesus says that it is not for him to do this, then he uses this opportunity to tell a parable about a rich man who is very pleased with all his possessions but who dies before he can enjoy them. The wise thing to do, says Jesus, is not to worry about worldly possessions, but to make sure you are rich in your relationship with God. There is more to life than food and clothes.

Jesus and the Woman Taken in Adultery

And the scribes and Pharisees brought unto him a woman taken in adultery; and when they had set her in the midst, they say unto him, Master, this woman was taken in adultery, in the very act.

(JOHN 8: 3–4)

One day when Jesus is in the Temple, some Pharisees and teachers of the Law bring to him a woman who has been caught committing adultery, the penalty for which is stoning to death. Trying to trap Jesus into saying something incriminating, they ask him what he thinks they should do.

As if he has not heard them, Jesus bends down and writes in the dust on the ground. Then he straightens up and declares that whichever one of them has never sinned can be the first to stone the woman. He bends down again to write something else on the ground. When he looks up, everyone has gone, except the woman. No one has stayed to condemn her; nor does Jesus. He simply tells her not to sin again.

The Return of the Prodigal Son

I will arise and go to my father, and will say unto him, Father, I have sinned against heaven, and before thee, and am no more worthy to be called thy son: make me as one of thy hired servants. And he arose, and came to his father.

(LUKE 15: 18–20)

Jesus tells this story to illustrate God's love and forgiveness:

'There was once a man who had two sons. One day, the younger son asked his father for his share of the estate. Then he went far away and wasted all the money on riotous living. Just when his money ran out, there was a famine in the country, and to survive he was forced to work, looking after pigs. He was so hungry, even the food he was feeding to the pigs looked good.

Realizing that even his father's hired workers had plenty of food to eat, while he was starving, he resolved to go back home. He knew what he would say to his father: "Father, I have sinned against heaven, and before thee, and am no more worthy to be called thy son: make me as one of thy hired servants."

And then he set off back home.'

The Prodigal Son in the Arms of His Father

But when he was yet a great way off, his father saw him, and had compassion, and ran, and fell on his neck, and kissed him.

(LUKE 15: 20)

Jesus continues his story of the young man who leaves home, wastes all his money and, starving, returns home repentant:

'While the young man was still a long way off, his father saw him coming, and immediately his heart was filled with pity for his son. He ran to the young man, threw his arms round him and kissed him. He was overjoyed to see his son again, and ignoring the young man's protestations that he was not worthy to be treated as a son, he called to his servants to bring the best robe in the house for the young man, shoes for his feet and a ring for his finger, and then to go and kill the calf that had been fattened up and prepare a feast to celebrate his son's return.'

Lazarus at the Rich Man's House

There was a certain rich man, which was clothed in purple and fine linen, and fared sumptuously every day; and there was a certain beggar named Lazarus, which was laid at his gate, full of sores, and desiring to be fed with the crumbs which fell from the rich man's table: moreover the dogs came and licked his sores.

(LUKE 16: 19–21)

This is a story that Jesus tells to some Pharisees because of their great love of money:

'There was once a rich man who lived in luxury, wearing expensive clothes and eating the finest foods. At his gate lay Lazarus, a beggar, covered in sores and hoping for a few crumbs of food from the rich man's table.

Both men died. Lazarus went to heaven; the rich man went to hell. In torment, the rich man saw Abraham, with Lazarus beside him. He called out to Abraham to ask Lazarus to dip his finger in water and bring it to him to cool his tongue, for he was being tormented by the flames. Abraham reminded the rich man that while he was alive he had all the good things in life, and Lazarus had the bad things. And now it is the other way round, and nothing can be done about it.'

G. Doré
A. BERTRAND. Sc

The Pharisee and the Publican

The Pharisee prayed thus, God, I thank thee, that I am not as other men are, even as this publican. And the publican, smote upon his breast, saying, God be merciful to me a sinner.

(LUKE 18: 11, 13)

This is a story that Jesus tells one day to some people who are very sure of their own goodness and who look down on everyone else:

'A Pharisee and a tax collector both went to the Temple to pray. The Pharisee was proud of his righteousness, and thanked God that he was not like everyone else: he did not cheat people, he was not dishonest, he did not commit adultery. He fasted twice a week, and he gave a tenth of all his income to God. He was certainly not like that tax collector standing over there.

The tax collector, on the other hand, stood at a distance, and would not even rise his eyes to heaven but beat his breast and begged God to have mercy on him for being a sinner.'

Jesus tells his listeners that it is the humble tax collector, not the proud Pharisee, who has put himself right with God.

Jesus Blessing the Little Children

And he took them up in his arms, put his hands upon them, and blessed them.

(MARK 10: 16)

One day some children are brought to Jesus for a blessing. The disciples are unhappy about this and rebuke the parents. This displeases Jesus and he tells the disciples to let the children come to him, because the Kingdom of Heaven belongs to those who come to it like little children: only a person who receives the Kingdom of Heaven with childlike innocence and trust will enter it.

And then Jesus takes the children in his arms and blesses them.

The Resurrection of Lazarus

And he cried with a loud voice, Lazarus, come forth. And he that was dead came forth, bound hand and foot with graveclothes: and his face was bound about with a napkin.

(JOHN 11: 43–44)

When Lazarus, the brother of Mary and Martha, falls ill, his sisters send word to Jesus to come. Jesus, however, does not set off for Bethany, where Lazarus and his sisters live, until two days have passed.

As they start out, Jesus tells his disciples that Lazarus is in fact already dead; and, by the time they reach Bethany, Lazarus has been in his tomb for four days. Mary and Martha both reproach Jesus, saying that if he had come sooner, Lazarus would not have died.

They go to the tomb, a cave with a stone rolled across its entrance, and Jesus gives orders for the stone to be moved away. Then, after prayer, Jesus calls out: 'Lazarus, come out!' And although he has been dead for four days, Lazarus comes out of the tomb, still wrapped in his grave-clothes.

The Entry of Jesus into Jerusalem

And a very great multitude spread their garments in the way; others cut down branches from the trees, and strawed them in the way. And the multitudes that went before, and that followed, cried, saying, Hosanna to the Son of David: Blessed is he that cometh in the name of the Lord; Hosanna in the highest.

(MATTHEW 21: 8–9)

As Jesus is preparing to enter Jerusalem, he sends two of his disciples ahead into the village of Bethphage, telling them that they will find a donkey and her colt tied up there. The disciples bring the ass and the colt to Jesus, and put their cloaks on them. Then Jesus rides into Jerusalem.

There is a large crowd of people along the way. Some spread their cloaks on the road, others cut down branches from the trees and strew them on the ground. And the people that go in front of Jesus, and those who are following behind, shout: 'Hosanna to the Son of David. Blessed is he who comes in the name of the Lord. Hosanna in the highest heavens.'

The Buyers and Sellers Driven out of the Temple

And Jesus went into the temple of God, and cast out all them that sold and bought in the temple.

(MATTHEW 21: 12)

When Jesus enters Jerusalem, he goes to the Temple. There he drives out the people who are buying and selling animals for sacrifice. He overturns the moneychangers' tables and the stools of the people who are selling doves for sacrifice, quoting the Scripture that says the house of God is to be a house of prayer, while the merchants have turned it into a den of thieves.

When the chief priests and the teachers of the law hear what Jesus has done, they begin to look for some way of killing him.

Christ and the Tribute Money

Render therefore unto Caesar the things which are Caesar's; and unto God the things that are God's.

(MATTHEW 22: 21)

Some Pharisees ask Jesus whether it is lawful for a Jew to pay taxes to the Romans. While apparently asking a sincere question, they are in reality trying to trap Jesus: if he says the taxes should be paid, he will lose his popularity with the crowd, but if he says the taxes should not be paid, he can be handed over to the Roman authorities for inciting people to break the law.

Jesus sees through their trick immediately. He asks someone for a Roman coin, and then asks whose face and name are on it. 'Caesar's,' he is told. 'Well, then,' says Jesus, 'give Caesar what is owed to Caesar. But don't forget to give God what is his due too.'

G. Doré

The Widow's Mite

And there came a certain poor widow, and she threw in two mites, which make a farthing.

(MARK 12: 42)

Jesus is watching people bringing their gifts of money to the Temple. Many of them are rich, and give large gifts. But then along comes a poor widow who only puts in a couple of small coins. Jesus points her out to his disciples, saying that her offering is in fact much greater than those of any of the rich people, since they have only given a fraction of their riches while she has given all she had to live on.

The Last Supper

And as they were eating, Jesus took bread, and blessed it, and brake it, and gave it to the disciples, and said, Take, eat; this is my body. And he took the cup, and gave thanks, and gave it to them, saying, Drink ye all of it; For this is my blood of the new testament, which is shed for many for the remission of sins.

(MATTHEW 26: 26–28)

Jesus and his twelve disciples are celebrating the Passover together. While they are eating, Jesus tells the disciples that one of them is going to betray him. They are all saddened by this, and each in turn asks Jesus: 'Is it me?' When Judas asks the question, Jesus replies: 'Yes, it is you.'

Then Jesus picks up the bread, blesses it, breaks it into pieces and gives it to the disciples, saying; 'Take this and eat it. This is my body, which will be broken for you.' And picking up a cup of wine, he passes it to the disciples, saying: 'Drink this. This is my blood, the blood that seals the new covenant, poured out for the forgiveness of sins, as a sacrifice on behalf of many people.'

G. Doré
BERTRAND

Jesus Praying in the Garden

Then cometh Jesus with them unto a place called Gethsemane, and saith unto the disciples, Sit ye here, while I go and pray yonder.

(MATTHEW 26: 36)

After celebrating the Passover together, Jesus and the disciples walk out to the Mount of Olives. When they come to a place called Gethsemane, Jesus tells most of the disciples to sit and wait while he goes off to pray, taking Peter, James and John with him.

While Jesus is praying, Peter, James and John fall asleep; they are so tired, they just cannot keep their eyes open.

G. Doré

The Agony in the Garden

And there appeared an angel unto him from heaven, strengthening him.

(LUKE 22: 43)

After celebrating the Passover with his disciples, Jesus is praying at Gethsemane. Knowing the fate that awaits him, he is overcome with anguish and distress, and prays: 'Father, please take this cup of suffering away from me. Nevertheless, let it be as you want, not as I want.' And suddenly an angel appears to give him strength.

So fervent are Jesus' prayers, and so great his agony of spirit, that his sweat falls to the ground like drops of blood.

The Judas Kiss

And as soon as he was come, he goeth straightway to him, and saith, Master, master; and kissed him.

(MARK 14: 45)

After celebrating the Passover with his disciples, Jesus has been praying at Gethsemane. He knows that Judas will betray him.

Suddenly, led by Judas, a crowd of men arrive, armed with swords and clubs. They have been sent by the chief priests and the teachers and leaders of the Temple. Judas has told them that the man he kisses is the one they are to arrest, so he goes over to Jesus and says 'Master', and kisses him.

One of Jesus' followers draws his sword and strikes the High Priest's servant, cutting off his right ear. But Jesus forbids any fighting on his behalf, and stretching out his hand, he touches the servant's ear and heals it.

G. Doré
PANNEMAKER DOMS

St Peter Denying Christ

And immediately, while he yet spake, the cock crew. And the Lord turned, and looked upon Peter. And Peter remembered the word of the Lord, how he had said unto him, Before the cock crow, thou shalt deny me thrice. And Peter went out, and wept bitterly.

(LUKE 22: 60–62)

When Jesus is arrested, he is taken to the High Priest's house. Peter follows at a distance, and at the house he sits down with others around a fire.

Jesus had told Peter that he would deny knowing him no fewer than three times before cockcrow. While Peter is sitting at the fire, a servant woman says she is sure he was with Jesus, but Peter's courage fails him and he denies it. Then someone else says: 'You *are* one of Jesus' followers', and again Peter denies it. About an hour later, a third person says: 'This man was definitely with Jesus', and yet again Peter denies it. And just as he utters his third denial, a cock crows. Jesus turns and looks at Peter, and Peter remembers what Jesus had said. And he breaks down and weeps.

Jesus Scourged

Then Pilate therefore took Jesus, and scourged him.

(JOHN 19: 1)

Arrested by the servants of the Jewish High Priest, Jesus is taken to Pontius Pilate, the Roman governor of Judaea. Having questioned Jesus, Pilate goes back to the Jewish authorities and tells them that he can find no reason to condemn Jesus to death, as they have demanded.

Seeking a way out of the problem, Pilate reminds the Jews that it is his custom to release one Jewish prisoner at the time of the Passover. He offers to release Jesus, but, stirred up by the chief priests, the crowd demands that he release Barabbas, a Jewish revolutionary who has been involved in a recent uprising.

So, not wanting to risk a riot, Pilate has Jesus whipped.

G. Doré

The Crown of Thorns

And the soldiers platted a crown of thorns, and put it on his head.

(JOHN 19: 2)

Not wanting to condemn Jesus to death, but trying to satisfy the demands of the Jewish authorities, Pontius Pilate, the Roman governor of Judaea, orders Jesus to be whipped.

After carrying out the whipping, the Roman soldiers make a rough crown out of thorny twigs and put it on Jesus' head, wrap a purple robe round him, and mockingly put a cane in his right hand like a sceptre.

Christ Mocked

They bowed the knee before him, and mocked him, saying, Hail, King of the Jews!

(MATTHEW 27: 29)

After whipping Jesus, the Roman soldiers put a crown of thorny twigs on his head, wrap a purple robe round him, and put a cane in his right hand like a sceptre. Then they bow down in front of him, and make fun of him, saying: 'Hail, King of the Jews!' And they spit on him and hit him about the head with the cane.

G. Doré

Christ Presented to the People

When Pilate therefore heard that saying, he brought Jesus forth, and sat down in the judgment seat in a place that is called the Pavement.

(JOHN 19: 13)

Finding no reason to condemn Jesus to death, Pontius Pilate has him whipped, hoping that this will satisfy the Jewish authorities. Jesus is brought out, still wearing the crown of thorns and the purple robe that the Roman soldiers have put on him. When the chief priests and the Temple guards see Jesus, they shout: 'Crucify him! Crucify him!'

After questioning Jesus once more, Pilate again tries to release him. But the crowd shout at him, saying: 'If you let this man go, you are no friend of Caesar's.' Pilate tries again, saying to the Jews: 'This man is your king. Shall I crucify your king?' But the chief priests reply: 'We have no king but Caesar.'

Realizing there is no way out, Pilate gives the order for Jesus to be crucified.

G. Doré

Jesus Falling beneath the Cross

And as they led him away, they laid hold upon one Simon, a Cyrenian, coming out of the country, and on him they laid the cross, that he might bear it after Jesus.

(Luke 23: 26)

Perhaps because Jesus has been so weakened by his whipping that he cannot carry his own cross, the Romans seize a man named Simon, a citizen from Cyrene in North Africa, who happens to be coming into Jerusalem at the time, and force him to carry the cross instead.

G. Doré
PANNEMAKER-DOM.

The Arrival at Calvary

And they bring him unto the place Golgotha, which is, being interpreted, The place of a skull.

(Mark 15: 22)

The Romans lead Jesus out of Jerusalem to the place of execution, known to the Jews as Golgotha and to the Romans as Calvary, meaning 'the Place of a Skull'.

Jesus does not go alone. He, Simon (carrying the cross), and the Roman soldiers are followed by a large crowd of people, and in particular by a group of women who weep for him. There are also two criminals who are going to be crucified at the same time.

Nailing Christ to the Cross

They crucified him, and two others with him, on either side one, and Jesus in the midst.

(John 19: 18)

When they reach Golgotha, Jesus is nailed to the cross. He is offered a pain-killing drink of wine and myrrh, but refuses it.

Pilate has a sign attached to the top of the cross. Written in Hebrew, Latin and Greek, it reads 'Jesus of Nazareth, the King of the Jews'. The chief priests object to this, and suggest that it should read 'This man said, "I am the King of the Jews"', but Pilate refuses to alter what he has written.

The Erection of the Cross

And when they had crucified him, they parted his garments, casting lots upon them, what every man should take.

(MARK 15: 24)

As Jesus is crucified, he says: 'Forgive them, Father, for they do not know what they are doing'.

Then the soldiers divide his clothes between them; but rather than cut up his robe to share it out, they throw dice for it.

Standing watching the crucifixion are a group of women, among whom are Jesus' mother Mary, her sister, Mary the wife of Clopas, and Mary Magdalene.

The Crucifixion

There they crucified him, and the malefactors, one on the right hand, and the other on the left.

(LUKE 23: 33)

Jesus' cross is erected between the crosses of the two criminals. The people stand watching, while the chief priests and the Jewish leaders jeer at him, saying: 'He saved others; so if he is the Messiah, God's chosen one, let him save himself.'

One of the criminals joins in the insults, saying: 'If you are the Messiah, save yourself, and us.' But the other criminal rebukes him, saying that while they are receiving the due punishment for their wrongdoing, Jesus has done nothing wrong. Then he says to Jesus: 'Lord, remember me when you come into your kingdom.' And Jesus says to him: 'I promise you that you will be with me in paradise today.'

G Doré
H. PISAN

The Darkness at the Crucifixion

And it was about the sixth hour, and there was a darkness over all the earth until the ninth hour.

(LUKE 23: 44)

About twelve o'clock, darkness falls over the whole world. For three hours, there is no light from the sun. The curtain hanging in the Temple is ripped in two. Then Jesus cries out: 'Father, I place my spirit in your hands'; and having said this, he dies.

The crowd of people who have been watching the crucifixion go back to their homes in great sorrow. But Jesus' friends, including the women who have followed him from Galilee, remain where they are, keeping watch from a distance.

G. Doré

The Descent from the Cross

Joseph of Arimathaea went unto Pilate, and begged the body of Jesus. And he took it down.

(Luke 23: 50–53)

When Jesus is dead, Joseph from Arimathea, who is a member of the Jewish council that condemned Jesus but who did not approve of what they did, goes to Pilate and asks for Jesus' body. Pilate is surprised to hear that Jesus is already dead, but after summoning the centurion in charge of the crucifixion and checking that it is so, he tells Joseph that he can have the body. So Joseph goes to the cross and takes the body down.

The Dead Christ

Then took they the body of Jesus, and wound it in linen clothes with the spices, as the manner of the Jews is to bury.

(John 19: 40)

Pilate gives Joseph of Arimathea permission to take the body of Jesus for burial. Joseph buys some fine linen, and then he and another man, Nicodemus, take the linen and a quantity of spices to Calvary. There they take Jesus' body down from the cross and wrap it in the linen and the spices, as is the custom for a Jewish burial.

PANNEMAKER-DOM

The Burial of Christ

And when Joseph had taken the body, he wrapped it in a clean linen cloth, and laid it in his own new tomb.

(MATTHEW 27: 59–60)

When Jesus' body has been wrapped in linen and spices, Joseph takes it and lays it in his own tomb, which has just been cut out of solid rock for him. Then he rolls a large stone across the entrance to the tomb, and goes away.

The next day, the chief priests and the Pharisees go to Pilate. Remembering that Jesus had said he would be raised to life again after three days, they are concerned that his followers might go to the tomb, take away the body, and then claim that Jesus is alive again. Pilate tells them to seal the tomb and place guards round it.

The Resurrection

And the angel answered and said unto the women, Fear not ye: for I know that ye seek Jesus, which was crucified. He is not here: for he is risen, as he said. Come, see the place where the Lord lay.

(MATTHEW 28: 5–6)

Jesus is placed in the tomb on the eve of the Sabbath. Following Jewish custom, nothing further is done during the Sabbath, but the following day at daybreak Mary Magdalene and another Mary go back to the tomb.

Suddenly there is an earthquake, and an angel appears. He rolls back the stone and sits on it. The angel's face is as bright as lightning, and his clothes are as white as snow. The guards are so terrified, they are like dead men. The angel tells the women not to be afraid. 'Jesus is not here,' he says. 'He is risen from the dead. There is where his body was lying. Now go and tell the disciples that Jesus is risen, and that you will all see him in Galilee.'

Still frightened but also filled with joy, the women run to tell the disciples what has happened.

G. Doré
H. PISA

Jesus and the Disciples Going to Emmaus

And, behold, two of them went that same day to a village called Emmaus. And they talked together of all these things which had happened. And while they communed together and reasoned, Jesus himself drew near, and went with them.

(LUKE 24: 13–15)

The day after the Sabbath, two of Jesus' followers are walking from Jerusalem to Emmaus, discussing as they go the events of the past few days. Suddenly a man joins them and asks them what they are talking about and why they are looking so sad.

One of the men, Cleopas, tells the stranger he must be the only person around who does not know what has been happening: Jesus has been crucified, but now his tomb has been found empty and some women are saying that he is alive. The stranger then explains to the men that all these things were foretold by Moses and the prophets.

Cleopas and his friend persuade the stranger to stay and have something to eat with them. As the man blesses the bread and gives them some, they realize that he is Jesus. And at that moment, Jesus vanishes.

The Miraculous Draught of Fishes

And he said unto them, Cast the net on the right side of the ship, and ye shall find. They cast therefore, and now they were not able to draw it for the multitude of fishes.

(John 21: 6)

One day Peter and some other disciples are on the shore of the Sea of Galilee. They go fishing, but after fishing all night they still have not caught anything.

When morning comes, they see a man on the shore, but they do not recognize who he is. The man calls to them, 'Have you caught anything?' and when they reply, 'No', he tells them to cast their net into the sea on the right-hand side of the boat. When they do, they catch so many fish they cannot haul in the net.

The disciples now realize that it is Jesus who is calling to them, and Peter at once jumps into the sea and makes for the shore, while the others bring in the boat pulling the net behind them.

G Doré
PANNEMAKER-DOMS.

The Ascension

And it came to pass, while he blessed them, he was parted from them, and carried up into heaven.

(LUKE 24: 51)

While the two men who have met Jesus on the road to Emmaus are telling the disciples their story, Jesus appears in the room beside them. He again reminds the disciples that everything that has happened to him was foretold by Moses and the prophets, and in the Psalms.

Jesus and the disciples then walk out of Jerusalem as far as Bethany. There Jesus blesses them. And as he is blessing them, he is taken up into a cloud so that they can no longer see him. Then two angels appear and ask the disciples why they are all staring up at the sky. 'Jesus has been taken up into heaven,' say the angels, 'but he will one day return the same way.'

The disciples then return joyfully to Jerusalem.

The Descent of the Spirit

And they were all filled with the Holy Ghost, and began to speak with other tongues, as the Spirit gave them utterance.

(Acts 2: 4)

Before Jesus is taken up into heaven, he promises the disciples that they will receive power by the Holy Spirit. They are to wait in Jerusalem until this happens.

Nearly two months later, at Pentecost, the disciples are all gathered in one place. Suddenly there is a noise like a strong wind, and what look like tongues of fire come down on each of them. They are all filled with the Holy Spirit, and begin to speak in other languages as the Holy Spirit gives them the power.

The Apostles Preaching the Gospel

But Peter, standing up with the eleven, lifted up his voice, and said unto them, Ye men of Judaea, and all ye that dwell at Jerusalem, be this known unto you, and hearken to my words.

(ACTS 2: 14)

When the disciples receive the power of the Holy Spirit, they begin to speak in many languages. Now, in Jerusalem at this time there are Jews from all over the world, and they are amazed to hear these people from Galilee speaking in their various languages, telling of the great things that God has done.

Some people laughingly say that the disciples must be drunk, but Peter says this is not so: they would not be drunk at nine o'clock in the morning. Rather, this is the very thing that the prophet Joel had said would happen: 'I will pour out my Spirit on all the people; and your sons and your daughters will prophesy.'

PANNEMAKER-DOMS

St Peter and St John at the Beautiful Gate

Then Peter said, Silver and gold have I none; but such as I have give I thee: In the name of Jesus Christ of Nazareth rise up and walk.

(Acts 3: 6)

One day Peter and John go to the Temple for the afternoon prayer service. As they come to the Temple entrance known as the 'Beautiful Gate', they see a man who has been crippled all his life being carried to the gate to beg.

Seeing the two disciples, the man asks them to give him something. Peter says: 'I have no money, but I will give you what I can. In the name of Jesus Christ, get up and walk.' Peter and John help the man up and, as they do, his feet and ankles become strong and he jumps up and starts walking. He goes with the two disciples into the Temple, walking and leaping and praising God. And everyone who sees him is absolutely amazed, because they realize that this is the man who has always sat begging at the Beautiful Gate.

The Death of Ananias

And Ananias hearing these words fell down, and gave up the ghost: and great fear came on all them that heard these things.

(Acts 5: 5)

As the Christian community grows, the believers share all they have. If someone owns land or a house, for example, they sell it and bring the money to the apostles, and it is shared out among those who need it.

However, when a man named Ananias and his wife Sapphira sell some property, they keep some of the money for themselves and give the rest to the community. Peter says to Ananias: 'Why did you let Satan persuade you to lie to the Holy Spirit by keeping back part of the money? It is not just people you have lied to, but God.' When Ananias hears these words, he falls to the ground and dies.

The Martyrdom of St Stephen

And they stoned Stephen, calling upon God, and saying, Lord Jesus, receive my spirit. And he kneeled down, and cried with a loud voice, Lord, lay not this sin to their charge. And when he had said this, he fell asleep.

(ACTS 7: 59–60)

Members of a synagogue, unable to beat Stephen in debate, bring him before the Jewish high court on trumped-up charges of blasphemy. Addressing the court, Stephen shows from Scripture that the Jews have always resisted God, and accuses the present-day Jews of being deaf to God's message, just like their ancestors. Their ancestors persecuted and killed the prophets who announced the coming of the Messiah, and now they have killed the Messiah himself.

What Stephen says to the court makes them extremely angry, but when he then looks up and tells them that he can see Jesus standing at the right hand of God, they drag him out of the city and stone him. Calling on God to forgive them, Stephen dies.

G. Doré

The Conversion of Saul

And he fell to the earth, and heard a voice saying unto him, Saul, Saul, why persecutest thou me? And he said, Who art thou, Lord? And the Lord said, I am Jesus whom thou persecutest.

(Acts 9: 4–5)

After Stephen's death, the church in Jerusalem begins to suffer serious persecution. The believers are scattered throughout Judaea and Samaria. One of those trying to destroy the Christian community is Saul, who goes to Damascus to search out and arrest Christian believers there.

But suddenly, as Saul approaches Damascus, a bright light from heaven surrounds him, and as he falls to the ground he hears a voice saying to him: 'Saul, Saul, why are you persecuting me?' Saul asks, 'Who are you, Lord?', and the Lord says to him, 'I am Jesus, the one you are persecuting.' Trembling and amazed, Saul asks what he is to do, and the Lord tells him to go on into Damascus where he will be told what to do.

All this time, Saul's companions are speechless, hearing a voice but unable to see anyone speaking.

G. Doré
A. Lign

St Peter in the House of Cornelius

Now therefore are we all here present before God, to hear all things that are commanded thee of God. Then Peter opened his mouth, and said, Of a truth I perceive that God is no respecter of persons: But in every nation he that feareth him, and worketh righteousness, is accepted with him.

(Acts 10: 33–35)

Cornelius, a Roman centurion, is a devout man who worships God. One day he has a vision in which an angel tells him to send for Simon Peter. So Cornelius sends servants to fetch Peter.

About the same time, Peter too has a vision, in which he is told that he must not consider ritually unclean anything that God has declared to be clean, regardless of what Jewish law teaches.

When Cornelius' servants arrive, Peter agrees to go with them to Cornelius. He now realizes that his vision was telling him that Gentiles are not to be considered unclean, and that righteous people of every race are accepted by God.

St Peter Delivered from Prison

And, behold, the angel of the Lord smote Peter on the side, and raised him up, saying, Arise up quickly. And his chains fell off from his hands. And the angel said unto him, Gird thyself, and bind on thy sandals. Cast thy garment about thee, and follow me.

(ACTS 12: 7–8)

Herod has Peter arrested and thrown into prison, intending to put him on trial after the Passover. The night before Peter is to face trial, he is sleeping in chains between two soldiers, with other soldiers on guard at the prison gate. Suddenly an angel appears, pokes him in the ribs to wake him up, and says: 'Get up! Quickly!' And Peter's chains fall off.

The angel tells Peter to get dressed, put on his sandals, and follow him. They pass the first guard post, and then the second, and then come to the iron gate that leads out to the city. The gate opens all by itself, and they pass through and out onto the street. Then the angel disappears.

H. PISAN

St Paul Preaching to the Thessalonians

Now when they had passed through Amphipolis and Apollonia, they came to Thessalonica, where was a synagogue of the Jews: And Paul, as his manner was, went in unto them, and three sabbath days reasoned with them out of the scriptures.

(Acts 17: 1–2)

Paul and Silas leave Philippi and travel to Thessalonica, where Paul teaches in the synagogue on three Sabbath days. Some of the Jews, especially many of the women, believe his message that Jesus is the Messiah, and a large number of Greeks who worship God also believe.

But some of the Jews who do not believe Paul's message gather together a mob of ruffians and start a riot in the city. They drag some of the Christians before the authorities, accusing them of breaking the law by hailing Jesus as a king. This has the townspeople and the authorities in an uproar. So, that night, the believers slip Paul and Silas out of the city and send them to the nearby town of Berea.

St Paul at Ephesus

Many of them also which used curious arts brought their books together, and burned them before all men.

(Acts 19: 19)

St Paul spends more than two years at Ephesus, teaching about Jesus and the Kingdom of God. For the first three months he teaches in the synagogue, but in the face of hostility from some of the Jews, he withdraws and instead holds daily discussions in a lecture hall.

God gives Paul the power to perform wonderful miracles. If even a handkerchief or an apron that has touched him is taken to a sick person, they are cured. After an incident in which non-believers try to drive out an evil spirit in the name of Jesus, and are themselves attacked by the man possessed by the spirit, people are filled with awe and the name of Jesus is greatly praised. Many people who have practised magic pile up their books and publicly burn them.

St Paul Rescued from the Multitude

The chief captain commanded him to be carried into the castle. And when he came upon the stairs, so it was, that he was borne of the soldiers for the violence of the people. For the multitude of the people followed after, crying, Away with him.

(Acts 21: 33–36)

Although warned in a prophecy that if he goes to Jerusalem, he will be arrested and handed over to the Romans, Paul is determined to go.

Once in Jerusalem, he goes to the Temple, where he is recognized and denounced by some Jews from Asia Minor. A riot begins. Paul is seized and dragged out of the Temple, and the Jews are about to kill him when the local Roman commander arrives on the scene with some soldiers.

Having arrested Paul, the commander asks the crowd who Paul is and what he has done. Some shout one thing, and others something else, so, unable to establish exactly what has happened, the commander gives orders for Paul to be taken into the fort. The crowd becomes so wild that, by the time they reach the steps, the soldiers have to carry Paul to protect him.

St Paul Shipwrecked

But the centurion commanded that they which could swim should cast themselves first into the sea, and get to land: and the rest, some on boards, and some on broken pieces of the ship. And so it came to pass, that they escaped all safe to land.

(Acts 27: 43–44)

Arrested by the Romans, Paul insists on taking his case to the emperor in Rome. On his way to Rome, the boat he is on is blown out to sea by a violent north-east wind off the coast of Crete. The storm rages for many days, and everyone thinks they are doomed. Paul, however, reassures them, telling them that an angel has told him that he and everyone else on board will survive the storm, though they will be shipwrecked.

Eventually, they see a coastline, which turns out to be Malta, and a beach where the sailors think they can run the ship aground. But the ship hits a sandbank and breaks up. Those who can swim jump into the sea and make for the shore; the others hold on to planks or other pieces of the ship. And they all reach the shore safely, as Paul had said they would.

H. PISAN

St John at Patmos

I John, who also am your brother, and companion in tribulation, and in the kingdom and patience of Jesus Christ, was in the isle that is called Patmos, for the word of God, and for the testimony of Jesus Christ.

(REVELATION 1: 9)

John has been exiled to the island of Patmos for preaching the gospel. One Sunday morning, an angel comes to him with a revelation from Jesus. He hears a voice as loud as a trumpet telling him to write down what he sees in a book and to send it to the churches in seven cities of Asia Minor.

The Vision of Death

And I looked, and behold a pale horse: and his name that sat on him was Death, and Hell followed with him.

(Revelation 6: 8)

Among the visions that are given to John on Patmos is one of a scroll that is sealed with seven seals. As the seals are broken one by one, various horsemen appear.

After the breaking of the fourth seal, Death appears on a pale-coloured horse, followed closely by Hell. They are given power over a quarter of the earth, to kill by war, famine, disease and wild animals.

The Crowned Virgin: A Vision of John

And there appeared a great wonder in heaven; a woman clothed with the sun, and the moon under her feet, and upon her head a crown of twelve stars. And she brought forth a man child, who was to rule all nations with a rod of iron.

(Revelation 12:1, 5)

In another vision, John sees a woman clothed in the light of the sun, standing on the moon and with a crown of twelve stars on her head. She is giving birth.

Suddenly a huge, red, seven-headed dragon appears, ready to devour the woman's child as soon as it is born. The woman gives birth to a son, but the baby is immediately snatched away from the dragon and taken safely to God and to his throne. This child is to rule over every nation in the world.

Then there is a war in heaven between the angel Michael and the dragon and their armies of angels. The dragon, who is actually Satan, is defeated, and he and his angels are driven out of heaven and thrown down to earth.

Babylon Fallen

And he cried mightily with a strong voice, saying, Babylon the great is fallen, is fallen, and is become the habitation of devils, and the hold of every foul spirit, and a cage of every unclean and hateful bird. For her sins have reached unto heaven, and God hath remembered her iniquities.

(Revelation 18: 2, 5)

In another vision, John sees an angel come down from heaven and light up the earth with his splendour. The angel shouts out that Babylon has fallen and is now the habitation of demons and evil spirits and disgusting and hateful birds.

Then another voice is heard, calling on God's people to leave Babylon so that they do not participate in her sins and share in the punishment she will surely receive from God.

H. PISAN

The Last Judgement

And I saw a great white throne, and him that sat on it. And the dead were judged out of those things which were written in the books, according to their works. And whosoever was not found written in the book of life was cast into the lake of fire.

(Revelation 20: 11–12, 15)

In this vision, John sees God sitting on his throne, and the dead standing in front of the throne. And books are opened, including the Book of Life, and the dead are judged according to what they have done, as recorded in the books. And anyone whose name is not written in the Book of Life is thrown into a lake of fire.

The New Jerusalem

And there came unto me one of the seven angels and talked with me, saying, Come hither, I will shew thee the bride, the Lamb's wife. And he carried me away in the spirit to a great and high mountain, and shewed me that great city, the holy Jerusalem.

(Revelation 21: 9–10)

John has a vision of a new heaven and a new earth, and sees the new Jerusalem coming down from heaven like a bride. An angel takes John to a high mountain to look at this new city.

The city shines with the glory of God, like a precious stone. It has a high wall with twelve gates, three on each side, which are guarded by twelve angels and have the names of the twelve Tribes of Israel written on them. The wall is built on twelve foundation stones, on which are written the names of the twelve apostles. The city is square, each side being about 1,400 miles in length, and it is as high as it is long and broad. The wall is made of jasper and the city is made of gold. Each gate is made from a single pearl.

H. PIS